Becoming
a Whole Family

BECOMING
A WHOLE FAMILY

John A. Huffman, Jr.

WORD BOOKS, PUBLISHER · WACO, TEXAS

First Printing—August 1975
Second Printing—November 1975
Third Printing—April 1977

Library of Congress catalog card number: 75–10093
Printed in the United States of America

To
my special Anne
who takes so seriously
and
carries out so delightfully
her responsibilities
as Christian, wife, mother
and
all-around person

Contents

Preface

In 1964, Anne and I committed ourselves to each other in a public marriage ceremony at the Hollywood Presbyterian Church. Surrounded by her California family and friends and mine from the East Coast, we promised to live together until one of us should die, no matter what would happen in between. We took these vows in the name of Jesus Christ to whom both of us had previously committed our lives.

We are now well into the second decade of our life together. Throughout the years we have had our share of plenty and want, joy and sorrow, sickness and health. There will be more of each in the future.

During recent months, Anne and I have paused to reassess our pilgrimage in becoming whole persons in the process of becoming a whole family. Daily we wrestle with what it means to be a husband, a wife, a parent, a child. We, like you, have our anxieties about the future, as both our marriage and the futures of our chil-

dren are exposed to the tough realities of
contemporary American life. Now that the romantic blush of youth's idealism has faded into
a more realistic confrontation with life's problems, we are discovering an ever-deepening
awareness of our own personal incompleteness
which breeds a greater daily dependence upon
the person and work of Jesus Christ, the objective truths of the Scriptures, the strengthening
of the Holy Spirit, and the encouragement of
each other.

As a family, we are ready to admit our failures. We have many needs. We don't have all
the answers. Yet we are learning. Wholeness is
coming as we discover more about ourselves and
God's dealings with us.

What I write is my endeavor to share from
God's Word and our practical experience some
principles which we are discovering and humbly
applying to our own lives. I have written in a
highly personal style, illustrating with life situations. All cases mentioned are true, altered
enough in names, geography, and circumstances
to protect identities. I hope that some of our
discoveries will help you to join us in becoming
an increasingly whole person in an increasingly
whole family.

1
Is Your Family in Trouble?

The family is ". . . near the point of complete extinction," predicts Ferdinand Lundberg, author of *The Coming World Transformation*.

Psychoanalyst William Wolf views the scene and comments, "The family is dead except for the first year or two of childraising. This will be its only function." And Margaret Mead insists that in fifty years the family as we know it will no longer exist.

Such predictions may seem excessively pessi-

13

mistic, but let's face it, the institutions of home and marriage are reeling under intense pressure. During the past few years we've witnessed some alarming trends which threaten our conventional family structure: Communal living and various forms of group marriage rode a crest for a time, and even though the influence of such life-styles is declining, the scars on society are obvious. In addition there is a growing acceptance of the temporary-marriage idea. The "until death do us part" concept is completely disregarded as couples enter the marriage relationship with no thought of permanency. "Serial polygamy" as a life-style—a succession of two, three, four, five, six, or more marriages—is becoming increasingly acceptable. Neither society nor the church seems to frown on marriage without commitment.

In similar fashion, the responsibilities of parenthood are being taken lightly by an ever-increasing number of mothers and fathers. Alvin Toffler, author of *Future Shock*, feels that it is not entirely ludicrous to anticipate the appearance of an advertisement at some future time which might read:

Why let parenthood tie you down? Let us raise your infant into a responsible, successful adult.

14

Is Your Family in Trouble?

Class A Pro-family offers: father, age 39; mother, 36; grandmother, 67. Uncle and aunt, both 30, live in, hold part-time local employment. Four-child-unit has opening for one, age 6–8. Regulated diet exceeds government standards. All adults certified in child development and management. Bio-parents permitted frequent visits. Telephone contact allowed. Child may spend summer vacations with bio-parents. Religion, art, and music encouraged by special arrangement. Five-year contract minimum. Write for further details.

Unbelievable? Maybe so. Far out? I'm not so sure unless something dramatic occurs to reverse certain dangerous tendencies that are clutching the throat of society.

At the opposite extreme are the optimistic visionaries who glibly parrot slogans and predict that all is well with the world and the family is moving toward a golden age of increased leisure—six-hour workdays and three- to four-day workweeks will provide "together time." Apparently, their philosophy is: The family that *plays* together, stays together.

Against this background of confusing and complex extremes, I want to take a close look at the Christian home and family, but it must be honest and realistic. We must admit that, even among our Christian friends, disintegra-

15

tion, heartbreak, and disappointment can wreak havoc. My wife, Anne, and I have received several teeth-shattering shocks during the past few years. One was particularly devastating, for Bill and Jane were close friends. Bill and I played golf together, and Anne and Jane were deeply involved in the women's activities in the church. We attended parties together and enjoyed many happy times in each other's homes. On numerous occasions I heard Bill witness to his faith in Christ.

Then to our amazement the lid blew off their marriage. After a time of trial separation there was a quick divorce. Just like that—it was all over. And as inevitably happens, the ugly story began to filter through our community: Bill had been leading two lives. Among other indiscretions he had been dating certain of the bunnies from a nearby Playboy Club. And then to compound our shock we learned that during the trial separation Jane became entrapped in a temporary love affair. Two broken lives—and these were our friends.

Tragically, there are countless Bills and Janes in our churches who lead double lives until an explosion lays it all out in the open. But I'm convinced that for each such incident that surfaces there are many people who go on day in and day out living in a marital hell or just apathetically existing together in an indifferent and totally meaningless relationship. Outwardly they witness to their faith and may even be hyperactive in the frenetic busyness of church life, but inwardly they are failures, leading double lives. One friend of mine, Ben Haden, has described their condition as "not bad enough for divorce, but not good enough to be called a marriage."

What is the problem? Frankly, I'm convinced that we have a distorted and lopsided understanding of what it means to live the Christian faith. In our preoccupation with leading men and women to salvation in Jesus Christ, we have neglected—even though unintentionally—an in-depth emphasis on the Scriptures. In being concerned about theological purity, we have neglected interpersonal relationships. And in the process of carrying out the biblical instruction to "win the world for Jesus Christ," we have forgotten the importance of providing for the needs of our own families.

Hidden away in Paul's letter to the young pastor, Timothy, is a statement we should memorize. It is just as important as the familiar John 3:16. In fact, if this statement is taken seriously, it will revolutionize your entire life-style. Paul wrote: "If anyone does not provide for his relatives, and especially for his own family, he has disowned the faith and is worse than an unbeliever" (1 Tim. 5:8).

These are strong words which bore in at a point of critical weakness: neglect to provide adequately and responsibly for everyone who is a part of our home and family life. Paul exposes our tendency to let outside institutions take care of those whom God has entrusted to us.

This verse says that if we neglect to provide for relatives, especially for our own immediate family, we have disowned the Christian faith and are worse than unbelievers. And Paul is talking about far more than the provision of food, money, or any other physical need. He is referring also to the spiritual and moral responsibilities we have to our families. It is interesting to remember as well that Paul was talking to Christians. And in pressing his point home, at various times in his writings Paul actually compliments the accepted heathen morality of his day as he chides his fellow Christians. For example, in Romans 2:14 he notes that there are many non-Christians who, even though they are completely unfamiliar with God's revelation of himself in Scripture, obey the moral law of conscience. Again, in 1 Corinthians 5:1 he states that many non-Christians would not stoop to the immorality of incest—a tragic cancer which was eating at the vitals of the young Greek church of Corinth. In his words to Timothy, Paul implies that there are unbelievers who take better care of their families than some of the Christians he knows.

This happens. I know one man who dedicated his whole life to evangelism, traveling tirelessly around the country conducting huge city-wide evangelistic campaigns. In the course of his lifetime he must have spoken at several thousand youth rallies, but in his zeal for others he neglected his own children and family. I remember he said on one occasion, "I will take care of the children of America and trust Jesus Christ to take care of my own children." Today this man is dead, and his children despise his memory. Some of them have even turned their backs completely on the Christ their father served.

Because I was raised in a minister's home, many of my friends are PKs. One of these friends, the daughter of a prominent Christian leader, commented bitterly during her senior year in college, "I don't even know my father. He's been so busy serving his God that he has had no time for me as a person." This girl and her husband have recently added their names

19

to the rapidly growing list of second generation Christian marriages torn apart by divorce— another broken home with shredded dreams.

Recently I heard a radio advertisement for a military academy that was trying to build its enrollment with this enticing offer: "Let us make a man out of your boy. Send him to us, and we'll produce the finished product." Now, that isn't quite as blatant as the advertisement Alvin Toffler suggested, but it panders to our neglect and our tendency to shove off on others the task of raising our children. To do the job we depend on the church, the public school, or the Christian school, and when they fail, we blame them instead of ourselves.

In similar fashion we have come to expect the government to assume all responsibility for the poor, the aged, and the sick. We leave to the church—our ministers—the spiritual care of others. The community is expected to pool its resources and provide education, frequently without encouragement or commitment from us, for our children from kindergarten through college. And local government, again without much help from most of us, is expected to take care of all community needs with its police force, fire department, and other public services.

Is Your Family in Trouble?

Each of these is important, but the problem is that we have become overly dependent on others to take care of our basic needs. We have come to expect local, state, and national government to provide, not only the essential services inherent to their function, but also those spiritual, social, and cultural values which are better provided in the home.

Without question, this is one of the major cop-outs of our day. The words of Scripture are stern and penetrating—there is no doubt as to their meaning: If we neglect our own family, we are worse than unbelievers.

God has established the family as the basic element in community life. Responsible living must begin in the home. No institution can take its place, and the duties and responsibilities of home and family life cannot be passed on to anyone or anything else—they are yours as a father, mother, husband, wife, child, or grandparent. Each one of us is held responsible by God for our own.

Our instructions as Christians are clear. Then, why the breakdown? That's a good question, and I've thought a lot about it. When everything is said and done, I really believe that the hardest place to live the Christian life is in the

21

home. It is here that we let the barriers down—
the masks come off. The real you and the real
me surface.

It is comparatively easy to act pious and
Christian for the few hours a week we're in
church, but the real test comes at home, doesn't
it? The Lord is the only one outside of our intimate family circle who knows about some of the
tense trips we make from home to church on
Sunday mornings. Getting our family up,
dressed, and out of the house is an agonizing
task colored with raised voices and frayed tempers . . . then I try to preach a sermon on love
and family relations!

I'm sure we've all had similar experiences.
Home is where our true selves come through—
it is here the lid comes off. And to some degree
this is understandable. It's good there is one
place we can really be ourselves, but at the same
time, this can be more than a little dangerous.
If we allow all control and restraint to be lifted,
those around us in the intimate family relationship will be bombarded with negative input, seriously affecting their understanding of what
it is to be a husband, a wife, a parent, a child.

It seems to me that as Christians, claiming
enormous resources in Jesus Christ, it is completely out of character to talk about "the peace

of God which passes all understanding" and
then lose our tempers and kick the children
around either verbally or physically. In the
home our children receive their truest insights
into who God is and what differences he makes
in the lives of people. Our families will get more
Christian or anti-Christian education in the
home seven days a week than in one hour of
Sunday school.

When I first knew Phil, he was eighteen years
old and would be graduating from high school
in June. He just couldn't wait to go off to college. Why? Because then he wouldn't have to
go to church any more.

Phil's father was a prominent deacon in a
Baptist church, and his mother was a leader in
the women's missionary work. Everyone in the
church looked to them as outstanding leaders
and model Christians. But Phil felt differently.
He had been exposed to eighteen years of brutal
fighting in the home. His father and mother
were vicious in their verbal attacks on each
other. About the only thing they seemed to
agree on was that Phil was no good. They ha-
rangued at him for his long hair and far-out
clothing: "You are an embarrassment to us in
front of our friends." Phil was fed up and
wanted nothing more than to be free from their

23

oppressive domination and their complete lack of sensitivity to him as a person.

It was interesting that when I talked with him, I discovered that he didn't expect his parents to be perfect. What he said was, "If only mom and dad could be honest and admit their failures. If only they could let their hair down a little bit in church, sharing with some of their Christian friends the tensions and problems they have in their marriage. Instead, they try to act so perfect in public—so much in control. It isn't the fact that they have problems that makes them so phony; it's because they live such lives of cover-up."

I suppose this sort of thing could be repeated over and over again. It does have a faintly familiar ring. Certainly, none of us is perfect. I don't write from the vantage point of being a successful parent but rather as one sharing the failures and successes of our own home and experiences. I believe there is great hope for the Christian home and family as the exciting insights of our faith and of the Bible are brought to bear upon relationships with those close to us. Marriage, children, the home should be one long series of thrilling adventures that bring new and rewarding experiences to each day . . . I believe this can happen.

2
What Christ Can Do
for Your Family

All this religious talk sounds nice if you are religious. But I dare you to show me one practical thing your Jesus can do for me in my messed-up family situation. Don't just say a pious prayer, and walk on. Show me something real!"

That blunt challenge forced me to do some serious thinking. Does Jesus Christ minister only to the spiritual side of man? Or does he have something to offer the complicated business of family living?

After struggling with those two questions, I am completely convinced that Christ is capable, available, and ready to do many things for each of us and our families if we'll let him. But for the sake of our discussion, let's examine just five things he will do if we open up our lives to him.

First, *Christ can give us help outside of our own resources.* If there is one miracle God performs every day, it is the creating of new people. I'm not referring to bringing new babies into the world but to the releasing of an explosive power within a person that can open up whole new dimensions of human experience. One of the greatest contributions Christ can make to your family is to give them a new you. What a difference this can make in every relationship of life! And I believe there's a deep longing in everyone to become a new person, for change that can bring new zest and purpose and meaning to life. For example, imagine how exciting it would be if we were suddenly freed from our conditioned reflexes, negative drags, and the limited thought-patterns which box us in! But that is precisely what Christ wants to do in our lives. The Bible says, "Therefore, if any one is in Christ, he is a new creation; the old has passed away, behold, the new has come" (2 Cor. 5:17). God is in the business of re-creating people. This accounts for such descriptive phrases as "being born again," "new life in Christ," "transformed by God's Spirit."

Unfortunately, there are a great many people in church today who are trying to find insights into Christian living but who don't even qualify to be called Christians. Apparently they have the mistaken idea that attending church—going through certain motions—will produce the desired results, but this of itself can only cause a paralyzing frustration. The Bible calls this "a form of godliness which denies the power thereof."

Jesus Christ sets an enormously high standard for living. Any attempt to apply his teachings to life without being remade by him will ultimately drive a person to a point of despair. My firm conviction is that no family can become a completely loving and creative unit of itself or in its own strength; without Christ we will fall short and become crippled with guilt as a result of repeated failures. A new you may really be the answer to a healthy and happy family life—not a new someone else, but a new you. Why?

If you reduce the Bible to its central message,

you will discover that everyone has been created by God in his image and loved very much by him. Since we are created in his image, we have the capability to make moral choices. We are free to choose; however, the Bible says that the first two human beings took advantage of their freedom by making a decision to go against God's will. The Bible says further that the entire human race has been affected and infected by the rebellion of Adam and Eve. At the moment of their decision to disobey God something went wrong with his perfect creation. The Bible calls it sin, an active or passive rebellion against God. You and I are caught up in this: ". . . all have sinned and fall short of the glory of God."

Deep within us is a tendency to go our own way, and that is what really causes family problems. Out of this inner rebellion against God's will tension emerges between husband and wife, parent and child. This inner rebellion, inherent in every life, must be put down through re-creation into the image of God.

The great affirmation of the Bible is that God loves us even though we are sinners, and Christ took the action through his death and resurrection to restore us to a right relationship with God. Through this restoration your family can have a brand-new you.

But, for this miracle to happen, you must receive Christ and allow him into your life. This takes an act of your will which says, "I am a sinner. I need you, God. I want you to transform my life. I place my trust in Jesus Christ and am willing to be remade."

Anyone who is willing to take this step or has taken it can be certain of Christ's help in both personal and family living. You now have resources of power which come from outside your own personal potentialities. You have the presence of God's Holy Spirit, an energizing, enabling, spiritual power and person. Also, the Christian can tap the power of prayer in which God will become intimately involved in the complexities of everyday family living. Actually there are over eight thousand promises in the Scriptures which are available to the believer in Christ—promises which do not apply to those who have not accepted him as Savior.

Jim and Marcia are their real names, and they've given me permission to tell their story. Their son, Doug, was born into a home filled with strife. Jim was just beginning his dental practice, and Marcia was going through the adjustments of her transition from competent secretary to mother and housewife.

Occasionally Jim and Marcia went to church,

31

and they tried to be good people. But somehow, they couldn't get a handle on their problems and came within an inch of separation. Anxious for Doug to have some religious influence on his young life, they began to attend a modest little church in Key Biscayne, Florida. There they met a young pastor named Lane Adams, who was not in the least embarrassed to tell this sophisticated young couple that they needed to be born again. After quite a struggle, they made the decision really to open their lives to Jesus Christ. They were converted as individuals and gave each other a brand-new partner.

There was only one thing wrong—both Jim and Marcia still had the same package of problems. Jesus didn't come in and miraculously whisk away their difficulties. Jim continued to be a head-strong, stubborn, young professional, and Marcia was still a highly independent young woman adjusting to the confining elements of motherhood. Then they realized that they had to be willing to work on those problems themselves. The difference now was that they could draw on Christ for help outside of their own natural resources. All thought of separation was blocked out, and their marriage was saved—with the help and strength of the Lord.

Today, over a dozen years later, Marcia is the

mother of three children and a partner in an exciting marriage. She has told me about two prayers that became her daily, private utterance to God after she and Jim accepted Christ.

Prayer One: "Dear Jesus, please restore my love for Jim." She doesn't hesitate to say that she had been questioning her love; their marriage had gone dead. Coming to Christ hadn't restored that love immediately. It took effort on her part as day in and day out she claimed the promises of God's Word, believing that this love could be regained. What had been deadened by the strong ego and selfishness of two people could come alive by the delicate, gracious influence of God's activity in those same two lives. And gradually, love became real once more for Jim and Marcia.

Prayer Two: "God help me keep my mouth shut." That was her big problem. Two quick-witted young people with razor-sharp tongues had developed a highly skilled manner of doing verbal battle. Her prayer wasn't, "Lord, help Jimmy to keep his mouth shut." No, she had learned to ask God's control for herself.

Today, Jim and Marcia make no pretense of a perfect marriage. There are still times when those egos get out of control and the tensions come back. Yet, they'll be the first to confirm that Christ can give you help outside of your own resources. Their growing, loving, communicating marriage proves Christ's capacity to repair and remake broken family relationships.

Second, *Christ gives a new look at marriage.* Not only do we have Christ's conversionary resources, but we also have the objective promises of the Scriptures and the strength of the Holy Spirit. Although it may come as a surprise to some people, the Bible gives specific instructions for home and family living.

For example, teen-agers who love Christ can receive positive guidance from the Bible about who and what kind of a person they should marry. The most important thing is not to be unequally yoked with unbelievers. Believe me, a lifetime of marital unhappiness can be prevented by not becoming involved in marriage with someone who does not share your love for Christ. This is not an easy decision to make. It will have an early influence on dating patterns. I've never known anyone to marry someone they haven't dated. If a Christian consistently dates non-Christians, the chances are very strong for an unequal marriage. And if that happens, the Christian partner will either have to sacrifice convictions for the sake of marital oneness or go it alone within the marriage relationship without being able to share a spiritual camaraderie.

Many problems will be solved if Jesus Christ is allowed to be the Lord of your social life. It may mean going without invitations to some important social events. It may mean gearing your social life to the church youth activities or to those of the Christian group in the high school or college. And in dating and courtship it will mean not only saying no to unchristlike social activities but to those personal drives that of themselves are of God but are meant for the marriage relationship. This kind of Christian discipline brings maturity—a sign of which is the ability to postpone immediate gratification for the ultimate good. In other words, saying no to certain social relationships now releases you to a higher quality of life later on.

Anne and I have fewer potential problems today because we are both believers in Jesus Christ. She was twenty-one years old and I was twenty-three when we met. It had been hard for each of us during those teen-age years before we met to say no to those things we believed Christ would have us avoid. There were doubts and questions and temptations all along the line; yet we were firmly committed to going God's way. Today each of us will confirm that God's way is best.

In addition the Bible not only gives instruction in the selection of a marriage partner, but it also stresses the attitude of permanence that is so necessary to a successful marriage. Two become one, 'til death doth part. This one-flesh concept runs diametrically opposed to society's understanding of marriage. Many people see marriage as a road to personal happiness, but the Christian who takes the Bible seriously sees marriage as the way to make another person happy. All too often we Christians allow our views to become distorted by a "happiness" syndrome. We find ourselves disillusioned if our partner fails to perform in a way that brings *us* ultimate happiness. To put *my happiness* first, to make *my happiness* the primary goal of life is contrary to the teachings of Jesus. The person who rates himself number one—above all others—is indeed a miserable human being. If you and I gear our lives to pampering our narcissistic, self-gratifying whims, we will be unhappy. The right order for authentic happiness is Jesus Christ first and your husband or wife second.

Third, *Christ helps us admit it when we are*

wrong. As Christians, we must be able to admit that we are sinners. When confession has been made to God, it is much easier to confess our faults to those with whom we live so closely. When we can bend our knees to God and say, "I'm sorry," our egos can survive that devastating blow of having to go to our marriage partner and say, "I'm sorry." Anne and I have been working on this and have made some progress in being able to apologize to each other. However, an incident which occurred some time ago impressed on me the importance of being sensitive and open and honest with our children as well.

Anne and I had been involved in some verbal fireworks. I had been overbearing and harsh. Normally, after a skirmish like this we would slip away to the bedroom, pray together, give each other a big hug and a kiss, and find that great release which comes from saying, "I'm sorry." But on this occasion I saw our little three-year-old, Suzanne Marie, watching and listening. Suddenly, it dawned on me that her ears and eyes were taking in something that wasn't good. So, this time instead of going to our bedroom with Anne, I turned and said, "Suzanne, Daddy's been a bad boy. Daddy needs a spanking, doesn't he?" Her eyes became big as saucers, but the shocked expression quickly changed to an ear-to-ear smile. Her response was, "Daddy naughty, too?"

I have a feeling that Suzanne probably thought she was the only naughty one in our family. After all, Mommy and Daddy never admitted they were wrong even though she had seen them do things that were wrong. For the first time, she realized a release in her attitude toward us as we honestly acknowledged our wrong. What a great thing it would be in our family relationships if we parents could be honest enough to tell our children we're sorry when we've done something wrong!

Fourth, *Christ enables us to back up another member of the family when he or she is wrong.* Once we understand our own sinful nature and can admit our faults, we're much more sympathetic to the faults of others. You know who you are; you know who they are. You can back them up in their failure, even as they back you up in yours.

One day an FBI agent spoke to the Kiwanis Club of which I was a member, and he gave a stem-winding talk on drug abuse. It was one of those tough, law-and-order addresses. At the end of his talk he said, "If I ever catch my son smoking marijuana, I'll grab him by the scruff of his neck, shake him until his teeth rattle, point my finger in his face and say, 'You're not my son.' " Do you know what we did? We jumped to our feet and gave him a standing ovation. That sounded great! That's the way to handle the drug problem!

Suddenly my heart sank. No, that isn't the way to handle a son caught up in drugs. In fact, that is probably the best way to cause him to get involved even more since it would communicate the insecurity of "I'm accepted only if I'm perfect."

I thought of my own father and an incident that occurred when I was ten or eleven. I threw a rock at a friend, and while it missed him, it went through the front window of a neighbor's house. Apparently, the neighbor recognized me as I disappeared around the corner and ran to hide in our basement. It wasn't long before the front doorbell rang. When my father went to the door, the neighbor said, "I think your Johnny just threw a rock through my window." My dad didn't respond with a "No, my son wouldn't do something like that; it must have been someone else." Not at all. He searched through the house and found me in the basement. Hauling me up in front of the neighbor, he asked, "Did you break the window?" And I had to admit it. Did he open his wallet and take out a ten-dollar bill, saying, "Here. Go get your window fixed"? No, he didn't. Instead he said, "Johnny and I will take care of fixing that window."

Together we went to the hardware store. Dad bought window glass, putty, and the necessary tools. We drove to the neighbor's house, and for the next couple of hours Dad and I worked side by side fixing that window. Can you imagine the warm feeling I had? My father had stood by me even when I was wrong. I felt the security of his love and care. After that I was far more careful than I'd ever been before because I didn't want to embarrass him again. For me this was an excellent example of how Christ stands by us and enables us to stand by others when they are wrong.

And fifth, *Christ helps us communicate the visible option of personal Christian faith to our children.*

We don't own our children. We have them at the most in our homes for a couple of decades. They are our responsibility during their growing up years. And a good part of those years is involved in preparing them to live on their own. What spiritual resources will they have when they finally break free from us? What can we do now to at least validate our confidence in Jesus Christ?

40

Looking back to my own parents I see two people who sincerely loved the Lord. They weren't playing games with their faith. It is true they weren't perfect, but they didn't claim to be. That's what always impressed me. They made their mistakes, and at least most of the time were willing to admit them. Sometimes they were pretty serious in their concern for our family welfare. We shed some heavy tears together. But the key was that those tears were shed *together*. We were a family.

I can't say that we were particularly successful at family worship. I've always wondered about those families who prided themselves in never missing devotions. Ours didn't function that way. Many evenings Dad wasn't home for dinner because he was out in pastoral visitation or at a church meeting. During my first fourteen years of life in Boston he had a six o'clock A.M. radio broadcast which made it necessary for him to leave home long before breakfast. But there was a spiritual center to our home. And Mother tried to lead us in family worship when Dad wasn't there. I remember many an evening when my sister, Miriam, and I would tease Mother with our giggling response to her serious efforts at Bible reading and prayer. When Dad was there it went a bit better. He was able to roll a bit more with our youthful punches.

However, the message got through. We knew Mom and Dad were serious about Jesus Christ. Together we shared our family needs in prayer. Far more important to me than a regular daily family worship, in which for a few moments we were religious, was the earnest tone of simple trust in Christ which pervaded our home twenty-four hours a day, seven days a week.

We had fun being Christians. Although Mom and Dad had strict standards, I don't remember ever sensing that they were majoring on minors. They knew how to keep the essentials of Christian faith and practice separated from the nonessentials. Even Dad's church duties never got in the way of his being a fun-loving father. He was always available to me as a person. I'll never forget those two and three A.M. sessions in Mom and Dad's bedroom when I wanted to talk through a teenage problem. Mother was always wide awake to help. And Dad, no matter how tired he was from the day's activities, would prop his head up and keep shaking himself to stay awake and hear me out.

This made a tremendous spiritual impact on me. These people called parents were *genuine*. They weren't religious phonies. Misunderstood by some outside of the family, as they had their share of problems, they came on as real people who were willing to give their very best to Miriam and me. Through our home moved a procession of missionaries and Christian workers. Some inspired the best in us. Others my sister and I considered unreal, overly pious, or just plain phony. But our parents respected our thoughts and let us express them in free-style communication which never put a lid on my personhood.

What came across? Jesus is real! He makes a difference. We could hear Mom and Dad praying together behind their closed bedroom door. And I can still picture Mom in her quiet organized way having her private devotions. Everything had its place. There was the well-worn Bible, her prayer list, the copy of *Streams in the Desert*, and another inspirational book or two. Hers was a quiet meditative life style. She was introspective with her Lord. Dad was just the opposite. He was as spontaneous as she was meticulous. Prayer for him hardly counted unless it was out loud. It was action oriented— usually done while driving the car. He never hesitated to pray in front of me—even about the most personal, sensitive matters.

Do you get what I'm trying to say? Jesus Christ does make a difference in a family. Personal faith can be communicated to children. I was tempted to tell about Anne's and my efforts at family worship—we've had some high moments and some that didn't come off so well—but I decided rather to share my impressions of what my parents communicated in their home. Anne could share a similar story of authentic family faith. It wasn't family worship that convinced me that Jesus was worth taking seriously. Rather it was the authentic personal faith "fleshed out" in the home that made the difference. I've viewed the other options. I've had my doubts. But frankly, the alternatives never looked too good because I'd seen real faith in action.

3
Meeting Your Family's
Material Needs

If any one does not provide for his relatives, and especially for his own family, he has disowned the faith and is worse than an unbeliever" (1 Tim. 5:8). This verse was printed on the stationery of the Presbyterian Ministers' Fund Life Insurance Company, the oldest life insurance company in America. What a convincing proof text for buying life insurance. But in rather blunt language it also lays down the rule that we are responsible for meeting adequately the material needs of our families. Economic considerations are biblically significant. Careful perusal of the Scriptures alerts us not to be so heavenly minded that we are of no earthly good.

In proper perspective *things* are important. Christianity doesn't minimize material needs. Christ made constant reference to God's material provision. Both the Old and New Testament records give a historical account of how God has taken care of his own.

Unfortunately, extremists have led people in false directions. On one hand the hedonists pamper every little sensual appetite and devote their primary energies to satisfying material whims. On the other hand the ascetics make a religious appeal to self-denial. Both hedonism and asceticism are perversions of how God wants us to live. As believers in Christ we live in constant tension between concern, no concern, or overconcern in relation to material things. But actually the Bible has a great deal to say about our physical and economic existence. With this in mind, let's look at six penetrating questions related to the all-important task of meeting the material needs of the family.

Are you working hard?

In God's economy there is no place for a lazy

Christian. In the very early pages of our Bible we hear God saying to Adam and Eve, "In the sweat of your face you shall eat bread till you return to the ground." Thousands of years later the Apostle Paul in Romans 12:11 urges the Christian not to be slothful.

Within each of us there is an innate longing for personal fulfillment and achievement. In reality this is a part of our authentic Christian witness. But unfortunately in our time many people are satisfied just to get by, while others have drifted into the "world owes me a living" syndrome. Both of these attitudes stifle initiative and rob us of the satisfaction of accomplishment.

I have a friend in his early forties who is heir to one of the nation's large fortunes. He draws on a trust fund which provides all the money needed to care for his family's material needs. Many would think that he really had it made, but basically he's an unhappy man. Without the need or motivation to work, he dabbles around first in one thing and then another. Freed from the necessity of having to get along with people just to put bread on his table, he vents his personal unhappiness on business associates in a most insulting fashion. When the going gets tough, he just walks out. Of course, in this instance his family doesn't suffer materially, but the emotional pain is intense and damaging.

Years of living in Florida gave me some interesting insights into the importance of work, of keeping busy, to the human psyche. I saw many Northern businessmen move south after dreaming for years of a tropical retirement. Most of them were in their mid-sixties, still vigorous and full of life. But unless these men developed a productive avocation—something more than playing golf seven days a week—they tended to shrivel up and vegetate, addicted to the past and with no interest in either the present or the future. In the country club locker room I listened in on many conversations that were loaded with reminiscences of past vocational experiences. Double martinis lubricated melancholy musings of better days.

By contrast, there is Claud Ruch, another retired friend of mine. When Claud retired from Field Enterprises, he developed a lifelong hobby —watercolor painting—into a creative avocation. And in addition to his own painting, he teaches some art classes. All of this, plus his dedicated service for Christ and the church, keeps him busy. Claud is working hard even in his retirement and is making a positive contribution to society. But most important he is

a fulfilled human being. How different from
Bill, who will probably soon die from the boredom of golf and a succession of cocktail hours.

God calls each of us, irrespective of our stage
of life, to the stewardship of work. Through the
creative and productive use of our energies we
are able to provide for the material and the emotional needs of ourselves and our families.

What are your priorities?

Even as the Bible stresses the importance of
good, hard work, it also calls us to reanalyze
periodically our priorities. Dr. Richard Halverson of the Fourth Presbyterian Church in Wash-
ington, D.C., was the first to confront me with
this revolutionary concept. Top priority, for the
Christian, is commitment to Jesus Christ; second, commitment to your marriage partner;
third, to your children; and fourth, to your
work.

It would appear that on Dr. Halverson's scale
of priorities the place of work has been relegated
to an inferior role, but quite the opposite is true.
If you put Jesus Christ first, your partner
second, your children third, and your work
fourth, ultimately, you will make a much greater
vocational contribution. For example, so often

BECOMING A WHOLE FAMILY

I've had occasion to observe the tragic end of a career-oriented man who in the process of clawing his way to the top neglected spiritual concerns and failed to consider the needs of his wife and children. For ten or fifteen years he sprints ahead in his profession. Seven days a week his energies are concentrated solely on being successful. He makes it to the top, only to discover that he no longer knows his God, his wife, or his children.

The night that Anne and I first met with the pulpit committee of the First Presbyterian Church of Pittsburgh is still vivid in my memory. They asked me about priorities. I outlined this "Christ-wife-children-work" order. Nine sets of eyebrows were raised. Lips pursed as nine minds pondered. Then quick, sideways glances passed between them as smiles spread across their faces, authenticating the validity of this set of priorities. A man who puts Christ first, partner second, children third, and work fourth is a person who will ultimately make a much greater vocational contribution to society. Because his life is balanced, there's a much smaller chance that society will have to employ one more social worker to tidy up the mess he has made out of his domestic life. This kind of a person is plugged into his God, his family, and his work in a wholeness of living.

Several years ago Anne and I attended a Christmas party and dinner that had been preceded by a "happy hour." Since we have made a commitment to each other to drink nothing stronger than coffee, we are occasionally confronted with situations which would be quite hilarious if they weren't so tragic. In the course of the evening, a man in his early seventies, whom I had never seen before, stepped up to us, poked me in the stomach, and in a voice which clearly betrayed his recent familiarity with the fruit of the vine, said, "Hey, reverend, I've got something to tell you. I've made quite a bit of money in my life. In fact, I'm a millionaire a couple times over. I've given my kids everything. But you know something? Next to my wife, here, there's only one other creature in the world who loves me. That's my dog. My kids hate me! So, my wife and I have taken care of them! Tell the reverend what we've done, honey." His wife said, "No, you tell him . . ." Before she had time to finish, he was back into his story without ever stopping to take a breath. "Last week we rewrote our will. We are willing our home, our Lincoln Continental, the services of our chauffeur, and all that it takes to keep up our home to our dog."

What a vivid example of a man with misplaced priorities. He had succeeded in providing every material advantage for his family, but in the process he had totally neglected their spiritual and emotional needs with the result that his children were completely alienated.

What kind of model are you?

People learn from models. Much of what you do has been learned from watching other people. If you have been fortunate enough to understudy a successful businessman, you have probably found yourself copying his methods and life-style. And right now, someone is copying you. Children learn more from our performance than from what we tell them. They adopt our attitudes and our values.

For example, our children's attitude toward money is derived from us. If they know that our commitment to Christ is so strong that we tithe —give 10 percent before taxes to the work of Jesus Christ—they will respect the seriousness of our commitment. Even if they choose never to tithe, there will always be that haunting sense of remembering that mom and dad put their money where their profession of faith was.

This same principle certainly applies as well to putting aside a percentage of your income for future emergencies. How can we expect our children to learn the art of proper money stewardship unless we set a careful and wise example?

But in considering the importance of providing adequately for the material needs of our families, we must not focus entirely on money. What kind of habits do we model? Do you exercise and watch your diet? Are you a good steward of the physical resources God has given you? Do you smoke? That's usually a touchy question. But an article in *Alive and Well*, a new health magazine, highlights this significant fact: "The primary reason for youngsters taking up the smoking habit is not magazine advertising, movies, or smoking friends. It is smoking by parents . . ." The article goes on to point out that the chances of developing lung cancer are twenty times greater for cigarette smokers than for nonsmokers. And finally, the article discusses the financial cost: If the amount spent for one package of cigarettes a day for forty years was invested at 8 percent interest and compounded monthly, the total would be fifty-six thousand dollars. This one example illustrates the significance of modeling well for those who look to us.

Are you prepared for tough times?

In all the emphasis on providing for our own, we have to face the fact that there are recurrent times of economic reversal. Seldom does a family make it through without economic strains. Reversal is a fact of life, but, if there is a pattern of diligent work, the difficult times don't hurt permanently. Actually, it seems that during periods of stress the family pulls together closer and lessons are learned that could come at no other time.

For example, I remember a little church my father served for eighteen years in Cambridge, Massachusetts. During the 1940s he sold his car to pay the church fuel bill. For the better part of a year, he rode his bike or took the bus to work. These were difficult times, but our family rallied around and helped in every way we could. Frankly, I probably learned more about money and sincerity of purpose in the bad times than in the good. I had my paper routes and worked as a caddy at the golf course. And I was encouraged to be an entrepreneur as I worked my way through high school, college, and seminary. For me, at least, the hard times brought learning experiences I value greatly today.

For some, this may seem an old-fashioned ethic, but I'm firmly convinced that God will bless our faithfulness and diligence whether the result of our effort produces a great deal of money or just a little. And I know from personal experience that he helps us bridge the periods of stress and hardship.

What is your attitude toward your partner's work?

I know a couple who overextended themselves to buy a beautiful home in a lovely suburb. Even though the husband earned pretty good money, the strain of monthly payments and taxes just didn't leave enough to match the economic lifestyle of their neighbors. They couldn't afford to join the proper clubs or take the "in" vacations. So now the wife nags her husband constantly about his failure to provide. Her ideals are too high. She doesn't realize that she's the envy of some whose husbands don't do quite as well. In the process she is missing the enormous blessing of God upon her life, and they are miserable because of her failure properly to appreciate her husband's efforts. It is so easy to latch onto a wrong set of values and lose sight of the importance of what your marriage partner is really achieving.

And the shoe is often on the other foot. We men are frequently guilty of a lack of appreciation and understanding of everything that our wives do. Just imagine preparing three meals a

day for the family, washing dishes, cleaning the
house, doing the laundry, taking care of the
kids. There's a lot more involved here than a
forty-hour workweek! Most of us would wear
out trying to keep up with our wives, but I
wonder . . . how often do we remember to say
thank you and I love you? What a difference
that attitude would make to our marriage and
family life.

What are you doing for your parents?

Paul writes, "If a widow has children or
grandchildren, let them first learn their religious duty to their own family and make some
return to their parents; for this is acceptable
in the sight of God" (1 Tim. 5:4). Charity begins at home. E. K. Simpson has said, "A
religious profession which falls below the standard of duty recognized by the world is a
wretched fraud." Secular writers have empha-
sized our responsibilities toward our parents to
make material provision for them. Philo wrote,
"When old storks become unable to fly, they
remain in their nests and are fed by their children, who go to endless exertions to provide their
food because of their piety." He noted that even
the animal creation acknowledged its obligation

to aged parents. How much more should we, as Christian men and women.

Our attitude toward our parents as they grow older is crucial in terms of our Christian life and responsibility. During our early years we were enormously dependent upon them. It is very possible that during their later years their dependence upon us will increase. This dependence may be emotional and spiritual rather than financial, but either way, feelings of mutual respect, love, and being needed become increasingly acute. One true sign of Christian health and grace is a loving response to both the emotional and financial concerns of our parents as they grow older.

4

The Four Basic Emotional Needs
of Those You Love—
And How to Provide
for Them

Dr. Armand Nicholi of Harvard University is one of the most articulate psychiatrists in America today. As a result of extensive research, he has concluded that the emotional response of today's student is rooted in his early home life. I believe you will find this fairly lengthy emotional profile of some modern youth helpful:

"One finds that many youth come from homes in which the family unit has virtually disinte-

grated. Uninvolved and absent parents, especially the father, give rise to repeated feelings
of rejection and resentment.

"The time demands on a highly successful
father, or even on the many less successful fathers holding two jobs, result in homes virtually
without paternal figures. In addition, the hours
that a mother spends at home and the quality
of relationship between mother and child con-
tinue to decline. When the parents do stay home,
the television set and other electronic gadgets
continually interfere with meaningful personal
relationship.

"In addition, the failure to set limits intensi-
fies feelings within the child that the parent is
uninvolved and uncaring, and leaves a residue
of poor impulse control and an inability to delay
gratification. The tendency to punish by with-
drawal of attention and affection merely adds to
the sense of being unacknowledged and rejected.

"Finally, in many of the more affluent homes,
parents send the child away to boarding school,
adding to the long series of traumatic experiences of rejection.

"In short, the particular orientation of modern society produces fragmented families, with
material values superseding ethical and spiritual

values, and with parents confused as to limits and basic priorities. This may be related to why many of the young reject not only the materialism of our society, but the entire free enterprise system as well.

"Out of this background comes the specific emotional conflicts that trouble young people today. Rejection inevitably gives rise to resentment and anger. The suspiciousness and intense anger with authority—always present to some degree in this age group—has now become considerably more intense, considerably closer to the surface, and considerably more difficult to control. Secondly, clinical problems reflect not excessive control and inhibition as in the past, but rather an inability to control impulses and to delay gratification. Thirdly, and more important of all, today's youth possess a peculiarly intense sensitivity to remote, invisible, and unresponsive authority—a direct result of early experiences with remote, unresponsive, and emotionally uninvolved (and often absent) parents."

I share this quote from Dr. Nicholi to emphasize the need of developing a healthy emotional climate in the home. When the Bible instructs us to provide for our own, I believe the reference takes in more than material and spiritual provision. It also charges us with making careful emotional provision for our families.

In our consideration of this vital subject, let's first examine four of our most basic emotional needs.

Every person needs an *intimate response*. This involves tenderness, sensitivity, and appreciation of the special nature of one's personhood. While we may at times be quite sensitive to this need in others, for some strange reason that sensitivity is not carried over into the family relationship.

I have noted my own weakness at this point. As a pastor I spend hours talking with all sorts of people about their problems—encouraging them to a wholeness in Christ. Such times are enormously rewarding, but after a full day of listening to and sharing in the deep emotional concerns of a wide variety of people, I find myself exhausted and drained. Driving home from the church, I try to relax and sort out my feelings in preparation for a quiet evening. Then I pull into my driveway and am confronted with a massive array of wagons, bicycles, and toys scattered crazily all over the place. My two daughters, Carla Lynne and Suzanne Marie, have a special gift for dragging everything they own from its proper place and then abandoning it right in the middle of the driveway. Time after time, I have pompously instructed Anne to make certain that the kids put their toys away before I come home from work. And time after time, these instructions have apparently gone unheeded. So, there is only one thing left for me to do; climb out of the car, pick up all of the toys and vehicles, and deposit them in their proper places. Then, and only then, am I able to put my own car into the garage. Believe me, after a routine like that my disposition is stormy, and the atmosphere when I finally get into the house is pretty dark. My emotional response to Anne and the girls is far from pleasant. And of course I haven't done or said anything that would stimulate a very happy response on their part either.

Fortunately, I have a wife who is sensitive and works hard at meeting my emotional needs. I remember storming in one night all steamed up over the fact that the toys hadn't been put back in their places. Anne was busy in the kitchen, but she listened patiently as I sounded off with my recital of complaints. Instead of tossing back a similar list of things that had gone wrong in her day, she just looked at me, smiled, and blew me a light kiss. At first I felt terribly deflated, but then I began to relax. Her intimate response to both the valid and invalid aspects of my frustration brought me into a brand-new world of peace with myself and with the ones I love the most.

Sometimes the harshest and most belligerent attitudes expressed by a family member are cover-ups of his own weakness, vulnerability, or personal need. Your sensitivity, tenderness, and love can release your loved ones to joy and peace as you are sensitive to their need for intimate response.

The other day a minister's son friend of mine opened up and shared some youthful wounds. He told how beloved his father was in the church and community. "I loved to be with my dad when he made his rounds. Everyone treated him with such respect. He was the life of the party. So much fun. Yet he was a different man at home. I never saw him show the least bit of affection toward Mom." And then haltingly he said, "And never once did he ever tell me that he loved me. I'm convinced that each of us children today bears some emotional scar from his lack of expression."

What is there that makes it so hard to say "I love you"? Why is it so difficult to show nonexploitive, genuine affection? I'm sitting here thinking about what I've said and written. I'm stung by my friend's account. While I'm pretty good at expressing affection to Anne and the children, I can't remember the last time I told my parents that I love them. I just picked up the phone and called them in Florida. Why? Just to say, "I love you, Mom and Dad." What a phony I am at times.

But words—as meaningful as they are, are cheap. Now I've got to get back to work thinking of ways to show my love. It's the little actions of tenderness which really count.

Four-year-old Carla Lynne just started crying. It's now eleven P.M. I put down my pen and went in to calm her. Usually Anne does that. She had to go "tinkle." So I took her. Then I crawled into bed with her for a few minutes. As I rubbed her back, she went back to sleep. And I lay there thinking and praying, "God, while I'm so busy writing this book about the family —keep me sensitive to mine! Thank you for little Carla. What fantastic potential for good or evil is cuddled here in my arms. Help me to treat her as a person. Help me to love her more. Help me to adapt my schedule to hers, letting her see how important she is. Help me to help her become a whole person in an increasingly whole family.

And what I pray for her I pray for Suzanne Marie sprawled out there sleeping in that other twin bed. Stand by her in school tomorrow. Convince her of your love. Help her to know you personally. And dear Lord, the same for our new little baby!"

Back to the manuscript tomorrow!

Second, there is the need for *adventure.* Everyone shares the need for adventure, and your loved ones are no exception. No life is emotionally whole without a sense of expectancy. All of us can look back and recall times when our expectancy levels were soaring: The first twenty dollars we made selling magazines . . . that love letter that finally came after days of agony and waiting . . . that first day behind the desk on a new job. These were times of eager anticipation, of excitement, of adventure.

Unfortunately, far too many of us have succumbed to a plain vanilla routine. There's no excitement, no joy, no enthusiasm. Every day has its set agenda, its static life-style. People caught in this milieu are completely predictable —and dull. These are the living dead. But this is not for you and your family. Every day is meant to be new and exciting for your husband or wife or children or parents. Every day sets the scene for adventure; you need it and your family needs it. By the way, stop a moment right now and think about it: Are you planning anything that will bring adventure into your family life?

Our third basic need is for *security*. That's why Linus in the Peanuts cartoon holds so tightly to his blanket. Until she was four years old our Carla Lynne dragged her blanket behind her everywhere she went. It got dirty and smelly, but that didn't make any difference to her. And when we tucked her into bed at night, that blanket had to be right there, clutched in her little hands.

The security habits of our children amuse us, but we all have the same needs. Your security blanket may be your job and some of the fringe benefits which go with it. For others it may be a club membership or friends or sitting behind the wheel of your Cadillac or belonging to the right church or wearing fashionable clothes. All of these, of course, are only symbols which speak to the deep need for security we all feel and must have and must give to those we love if they are to be whole and fulfilled human beings. If your emotional need for security is not being met by persons, you will inevitably seek it in becoming attached to material objects.

The final basic need I want to mention is

71

recognition. You and I need to be singled out as special.

For several years I was a member of the Downtown Miami Kiwanis Club. One of the highlights of our year was a golf tournament with the Miami Rotary Club. We all looked forward to the golf game itself, but the evening banquet was really the climax of the event. This was recognition time; awards were presented to the best golfer, the winning team, the worst golfer, the oldest, the youngest, the best-dressed, the worst-dressed. Everyone received an award, and it was fun to walk up and be given a dozen golf balls or even a can of bug repellent.

This same club did another nice thing which we all enjoyed. One meeting day a month was set aside for the recognition of birthdays. We would have a party, and all of the men who were celebrating birthdays that month had their own individual cupcake with a candle. The master of ceremonies would read out their names, tell a brief joke, and each man would light his candle while the other three hundred would sing "Happy Birthday." It seemed sort of "Mickey Mouse" to me eleven months of the year, but when my birthday month rolled around, I never missed the party! We all love and need recognition.

Joe Senior is a graduate of the University of Pennsylvania and Yale Law School. Joe Junior is seventeen. Joe Senior's dream is that Joe Junior will work into his law firm. There's only one problem: Joe Junior has no apparent aptitude for law. In fact, he has very little inclination toward academic pursuits of any kind. Joe Senior constantly rides him, trying to motivate him to academic excellence. He has used pressure, insult, compliment, and even bribery to achieve his goal, but nothing works.

On the other hand Joe Junior has a special talent. He can lift the hood of a car, take the engine apart, and put it back together again. He's a brilliant mechanic, but never once has Joe Senior given him recognition for his abilities. In his own way this young man is gifted—gifted by God! He, too, needs recognition.

Intimate response, adventure, security, and *recognition*—these are indeed needs we all share, and as members of a family we have an obligation in our relationship with one another to do everything we can to meet those needs. Let's look now at some practical suggestions as to just how this can be done.

Suggestion One—for husbands. *Why not try dating your wife?* You used to do it. If you're like the average fellow, it's been a long time since you called her up and asked her out. No, that business dinner doesn't count. That social obligation of a couple of nights ago when you went over to the Jones' isn't a date. Think back to when you were courting. The last thing you wanted was to go on a double date. You wanted to be alone together. There was adventure, security, recognition—and I dare say, a little bit of intimate response on those special occasions.

We wonder why some young people today say, "What difference does a piece of paper make? Why get married? A wedding certificate only seems to spoil romance instead of encourage it." While I believe they're wrong, they do have a point. They've been watching their own parents who seem to have lost the spontaneity of love. Life has become drab and routine and unexciting.

So, pick up the telephone, call your wife, and ask her for a date—just the two of you. Don't ask her where she'd like to go, but select a nice place with atmosphere. Make it special—a dress-up affair. Tell her how happy you are that just the two of you can be together . . . and that you love her.

I shared this suggestion at a clergy conference in Minneapolis last winter. Afterwards, a minister came up and said, "That idea of dating your wife is great. I never thought of it before. There's only one problem with it that scares me. I'm dead serious about this. I don't know what we'd talk about if just the two of us were together alone for dinner. It's been fifteen years since we've really been alone except for sleeping together each night. It's either the kids, the parishioners, or someone else who's always around. We don't ever talk any more."

Striking up a new romance with your partner will make you vulnerable. Your partner may even wonder what brought this change about. After all, it might be quite a transformation for you to suddenly get romantic—especially in day-light. You may have to pave the way with an apology for those months of neglect. I've had to do that. It's amazing how far a genuine apology can go.

Suggestion Two—for wives. *Think about what your husband likes best, and do it for him.* For example, what is your husband's favorite meal? When was the last time you cooked it? Did you tell him about it in advance? Or did you surprise him? Were you all dressed up when he came home from work? Five-thirty or six P.M. can be the most drab hour of the day. But it can also be the most exciting, when two people, who have worked hard all day, stop for a moment and exchange a kiss and a hug as a symbol of their oneness in Christ. You can help your husband relax by turning an average evening into a special time.

There's a great deal being said about sex today. Practically every newspaper and magazine has at least one article or story on sex. In fact the Bible has a lot to say about it. But, unfortunately, we Christians become very stuffy and unnatural when it comes to celebrating one of God's greatest gifts to human beings. True, sex can be exploited, abused, and degraded, but it is a gift of God which brings wholeness and gratification and joy to the marriage relationship.

Many books and articles are devoted to ways and means of turning your husband or your wife on sexually. This is all right up to a point because I believe we should be intensely sensitive to what stimulates and pleases our marriage partner. This is a part of selfless loving. But phoniness and manipulation are to be guarded against. True love doesn't use another person for personal gratification of any kind.

Just a brief footnote for both wives and husbands. Good sex begins at six-thirty, not ten-thirty. We men are probably the greatest violators in our insensitivity to this fact. We hide behind newspapers and box ourselves off emotionally from our wives before television sets. Then, at ten-thirty, we expect them to respond sexually. We wonder why they are cool, somewhat distant, and not eager to share in love. Anne and I have found that our best times together come when we have genuinely been making love in conversation, attitude, and sharing throughout the entire evening, beginning when I arrive home and continuing until we go to bed. Sex in its highest God-given dimension is the ultimate expression which says that the two of us love each other all the time. In this act of union we express the blending of our emotional, spiritual, and physical lives.

Suggestion Three—for parents. *Try dating your children.* A father in particular can benefit from this suggestion. I picked up this idea several years ago from Dr. Charlie Shedd. Early in his son Peter's life, Charlie Shedd took him to lunch each month so they could be alone and talk together. He continued this all through Peter's growing-up days.

I was so impressed with Dr. Shedd's enthusiastic endorsement of this plan that five years ago I started it with my own daughter, Suzanne Marie. She was two-and-a-half years old at that time. At first I thought I was crazy for even thinking I could have a viable conversation with a little girl that young, but I tried.

I called her up from the office and asked her out on a date. I had to explain that she should get dressed up, and I would pick her up at twelve-thirty. She was excited! She was all dressed up and waiting in the front yard when I arrived. We went to the Jamaica Inn, an English pub-style restaurant on Key Biscayne. After studying the menu carefully, pretending to be able to read it, she ordered a hamburger. Then we both leaned back, and much to my surprise, I discovered that a two-and-a-half-year-old can carry on an adult conversation when left alone with an adult. We had a great time, getting to know each other in special ways.

How exciting it's been during the past five years to have these dates with Suzanne, and now with little Carla Lynne. We're getting to know each other and are entering into a conversational style of life. It's true that I have to discipline myself to do it, and it takes time and energy. But, every time I come home from one of these dates I am convinced of the importance of being alone with each of my daughters. And now I can hardly wait until the new baby is old enough to go with me.

My father never read a book on this, but he practiced it intuitively. He had an arrangement with me that if I kept my grades up at school, he would take me on a once-a-year, out-of-town business trip. Ours was a strict school district —one of the first to prohibit parental-induced absenteeism. Dad took the bull by the horns, never faking illness, to accomplish his ends. He would write the principal: "Part of my son John's education is to be with his father. His grades are up to snuff. Next week he will be missing several days of school, accompanying me out of town on business."

As a result, I knew my dad. I still know him. He's one of my best friends in the world. Because of our close relationship, Dad never found it difficult to talk frankly with me about life. I recall so well a very explicit conversation we had one night when I was traveling with him in Cleveland, Ohio. I was only twelve years old at the time. We were staying at a hotel that was hosting a large convention, and that night the four men in the next room—which was separated from ours by paper-thin walls—had rented the services of a prostitute. We could hear everything that was going on, but Dad and I had a great talk as he described the beauty of his love and sex relationship with mother. How different

79

it sounded from the crude conversation and activity going on in the next room.

Suggestion Four—for children. *Try doing that job you know Mom and Dad want you to do without having to be asked.* A young friend of mine, who is nine years old, gave his mother a very special birthday present. The envelope said, "Coupons Redeemable for Taking Out Trash, and Cleaning My Room, Washing Car, Washing Dishes, Scrubbing Kitchen Floor for Mom." Inside there were fifteen coupons, artistically drawn by this youngster, each one specifying a particular job for which it was good. Was his mother ever turned on! The day after her birthday she showed me this little booklet of coupons with tears of appreciation in her eyes for her son's thoughtfulness.

The same mother shared a letter with me she had just gotten from her daughter who was away at college. Part of it read as follows, "On your fiftieth birthday, Mom, I want to wish you all the happiness you deserve. I'm so thankful that I've been your daughter because there's no one else I can think of who could have been a better mother for me."

Talk about meeting the emotional needs for recognition, security, intimate response, and adventure! These two young people made their mother the happiest in the world.

5

How to Get Along with Your Children— And Still Love Them

Columnist Janet Chusmir of the *Miami Herald* writes: "It has gotten so that I hesitate to ask about the children.

"I hesitate with friends because it will open wounds. And with strangers, because so often it ends up that I'm treading on their painful and embarrassing ground.

"Once, a woman I was interviewing brought the subject around to her daughter. 'I like my daughter. I respect her. I enjoy being with her,'

83

she said with such warmth and joy and enthusiasm that I—taken by surprise—wrote her words down in my notebook. Liking, respecting, enjoying a child . . . That was news."

Sylvia Herz notes that children are divorcing their parents at an enormously high rate. By this, she means that for some strange reason many children don't want to have anything to do with them. This goes for teen-agers. It also applies to many married people in their twenties, thirties, and forties who do not identify with their parents' life-style.

The Bible speaks to this problem in a way which can radically alter the relationship between parents and children—for the better: "Fathers, do not provoke your children to anger, but bring them up in the discipline and instruction of the Lord" (Eph. 6:4). In writing to the Colossian Christians, Paul words it a bit differently: "Fathers, do not provoke your children, lest they become discouraged" (Col. 3:21). The New English Bible translates those words, "Fathers, do not exasperate your children, for fear they grow disheartened."

From these words and from our own experience it is clear that we parents do at times agitate our young people to hostility and discouragement. And while in all probability this is unintentional, the results are just as destructive.

I'd like now to share a check list of four basic questions which can help revolutionize your relationship with your children. I'm not writing as an expert, but as a learner. I don't have all the answers. In fact, any expertise I have in this business of being a parent comes from being raised myself by two very wise parents. Of course, the ballots aren't in yet, and won't be for some time, on the job Anne and I are trying to do. Take what I say as coming from an experimenter who is willing to express his own weaknesses, fears, aspirations—one who is willing to grow with you.

Why not try these four questions on for size? When answered positively, they can help prevent the agitation of our children to anger, frustration, and discouragement.

Do I care enough to make any sacrifice for my children?

Just how far are you willing to go for the sake of your family? Often our concerns for our children are selfish. Yes, we love them, but we don't want to be burdened by their misconduct. We are willing to turn their care over to others in order to be free to do the things we like to do.

Mother, do you feel confined by the home? Are you yearning to break out of those four walls? Does the hectic activity drive you to despair? Do you idealize making a higher contribution to society by way of work outside the home? These are penetrating questions, and I'm certain there are moments when every wife and mother feels intense frustration. But I firmly believe that if you have children, your highest calling is to raise a happy, well-adjusted child who loves God, himself, and his fellowman.

Father, how about you? Are you frustrated by the demands of family living? Do you yearn for those bachelor days when you were free from the constant demands of being a father? Are you consciously or subconsciously endeavoring to avoid responsible leadership in the home? Is your work getting in the way? Is your recreation taking you away from your children so much that you hardly know them?

Several months ago, the "Today Show" carried a fascinating interview with Dr. James Windle, professor of management supervision at Purdue University. He was talking about his theory of the "I don't give a damn" syndrome.

He said there is a contagious attitude, rapidly spreading, in which people are paying less and less attention to doing responsible work. This is the reason your new car breaks down so quickly and requires frequent adjustments. It is also why the buttons are misplaced or missing on a new sport coat or dress and the lining is sloppily sewn. Dr. Windle is convinced that no amount of management efforts toward job enrichment, rotation, shorter workweek, flexible work schedules, and many of the other temporary solutions will actually solve the problem. Rather, it can only be solved when a person has a deep sense of commitment to his work. He must see it as a top priority, not just a boring routine to somehow provide bread for the table.

This same syndrome can apply so easily in our family life and in the raising of our children. We drift into an attitude of routine boredom and complacency, allowing outside interests to detract from and dull our relationships with husband or wife and children.

This is why we must keep emphasizing priorities. I must constantly remind myself that priority one is personal commitment to Jesus Christ. Priority two is the husband-and-wife relationship, and priority three, the relationship with our family. And finally, my fourth prior-

87

ity is vocation. Unfortunately, number four is so often placed at the top to the detriment of the others.

In confronting the awesome problem of caring for and being responsible for our children, we may be called upon to make hard personal sacrifices in terms of our economic and social life. We may come to see that our life-style and social relationships have a derogatory effect on the attitudes of our children. If this happens, we ought to be willing to make whatever changes are necessary.

Friends of ours are going through this struggle right now. Their attractive and vivacious thirteen-year-old daughter is beginning to run with the wrong crowd in the highly affluent suburb where they live. Presently they have to drive quite a distance in order to attend a spiritually vital, Christ-serving, evangelical church. But now they're considering selling their beautiful home and moving closer to the church so their daughter can be more intimately involved in all of the activities and with the right kind of young people. Such a move will call for temporary hardship and sacrifice, but for them, the spiritual care of their daughter comes first.

My in-laws were willing to sacrifice for their daughters. Instead of comfortably attending a neighborhood church close at hand, they scoured Los Angeles until they found the finest evangelical Sunday school setting for their children. Then for two decades they spent the better part of whole days driving their children back and forth the twenty plus freeway miles between their Westwood home and the Hollywood Presbyterian Church youth activities. They wouldn't take anything for granted. Their own comfort was incidental to their children's spiritual welfare. Anne's mother worked in the Sunday school herself. And her father became heavily involved as a board member of the Forest Home Christian Conference Center—so determined was he that his children and those of others would have this exciting spiritual influence. How different from those who don't take these responsibilities seriously enough to pay a price.

In my judgment, not really to care enough to make whatever sacrifice you're called on to make is to provoke your child to wrath, to agitate him or her to the point of rebellion or discouragement.

Do I take my child seriously as a person?

Really now, how much attention do you pay to your children? Do you view them as a group?

Or are you involved with them as individuals? On the surface these questions may sound a bit silly, but stop for a minute and reflect. Do you really know each of your children—what they think, how they feel, where they hurt? Do you spend time alone with each of your children as an individual? How often do you spend some time alone with each child building the bridge of personal understanding and personal relationship so he feels free to talk and confide in you as a person rather than a parent? In these moments alone we can talk of our love and caring and responsibility to each other. It is so easy to become so caught up in the family group idea (and that is important) that we lose sight of the need for that personal touch and understanding with each person individually.

One thing I am discovering is the importance of being available on my child's time schedule, not just my own. I've come to realize that my children are not always ready for me when I'm ready for them, and sometimes the reverse is equally true. Dr. Charlie Shedd relates an incident between his four-year-old daughter, Karen, and himself. He was getting ready to leave for an important church committee meeting and had promised the committee chairman that he would meet him early. As he rushed toward the front door, Karen called out, "Daddy, will you

90

read to me?" Dr. Shedd tells how the usual excuses started to build up, but looking into her eyes, he said, "Sure, honey, I'll read to you." So he stopped and read. It didn't take more than three minutes to read the story. Then he closed the book and said, "Gee, that's an exciting story. I can hardly wait to see how it comes out. Do you think you can wait?" "Oh," bubbled Karen, "I already know how it comes out. Mommy reads that one all the time." Reflecting on this incident, Dr. Shedd says, "How blind can a daddy be? Karen didn't want to know what the book said. The information she wanted was something else. She wanted to know that she mattered more to her daddy than some dumb old meeting."

When was the last time you crawled into your child's skin? When was the last time you identified with the kind of thoughts going on within that teen-ager who is in the turmoil of becoming an adult? When was the last time you took his romantic problems seriously? When was the last time you viewed her symbols of status—perhaps a pair of Levis, a pair of sandals, or a body shirt—as seriously as you take yours? We need to see our children as people who have a right to know what we are thinking and why we are so firm about some things. Don Shula, coach of the Miami Dolphins, says this about his relationship with individual football players: "The word I stress is 'communication.' I try to always keep the doors of communication open. Then when you do make a decision, players will accept it more readily than they would if you are dogmatic. They tend to reject dogma. I did as a player."

Our children want to know why. They want to see the real us. They don't want dogma—they want real, personal sharing. Child expert Dr. Bruno Bettelheim was once asked why so many parents don't like their children. His response was that the problem is not one of parents and children not liking each other. Instead, it is that "they don't know each other."

To fail to see my children as individual persons who need individual attention is to provoke them to wrath, to rebellion. And some day they will cry out, "I'm *me*. Care about *me!*" This cry for attention may not come in words and sounds you can hear. Rather it may come through actions which demand that you take them seriously, showing them the attention they need.

Do I respect the privacy of my children's personhood?

Taking a person seriously not only involves

giving him undivided, individual attention, but it also means sensitizing yourself to his need for privacy to become the kind of person he is meant to be. While it is enormously important to give our children the personal attention they need, there is a fine line that must not be crossed between that and smothering them. The over-zealous, smothering parent usually has intensely selfish motives: the determination to mold the child into a preconceived style of life acceptable to the parent.

But it's important to let the real child—the real person—develop. Sometimes we act as if we want to create robots, carbon copies of ourselves or someone else. We point to some other young person in school or church and single him out as an example. "Why can't you be like Johnny Jones? He's such a good, hard worker and courteous. He always looks neat."

How does it feel when someone tries to squeeze you into his mold? It's not very comfortable, is it? What is your reaction when your husband asks, "Why don't you dress like ——————" and names that one person you just can't stand? Or how does it feel when your wife compares what you provide materially—the car, home, furniture, and status—to what that other fellow gives his wife? Our children respond in the same way. They are individual creations of God with all kinds of creative potential. At this point I'd like to suggest a new eleventh commandment: "Thou shalt not frustrate the holy in thy child!" Isn't that really what the Apostle Paul is saying?

I believe our most difficult task as parents is to let the real person develop in our children. We want to manage things and shape them our way. In *Promises to Peter* Charlie Shedd says that one of the first jobs of a parent is to be able to say and mean: "Listen to me, children! Your first loyalty is not to me. You came by me, but you are not from me. In you there is a native self. The secret is to discover who God wants you to be and be true to that. This moment I set you free to say, 'Get off my back. I've got to be me!' "

Now this doesn't mean giving your child too much freedom. Every child needs rules. But it does mean being responsive to the development and growth of your child. Frankly, I believe the goal of parenthood should be to respect the personhood of our children to the point that at the age of eighteen they're capable of making the major decisions of life for themselves. Hopefully, with our counsel, they will mature enough to become adults. At the same time, though, it is essential to remember that this kind of maturity is only possible when we've given them careful guidance at each stage of their growth. I'm afraid that too many teen-agers today are suffering from an overdose of self-government.

In another of his books Charlie Shedd quotes a letter from a fourteen-year-old girl who was suffering from too much freedom. She wrote, "My problem is probably one you don't hear much. My daddy is a doctor and he is so busy. My mother is a champion golfer and she is at the club every afternoon when I come home from school. On weekends they party and sometimes I worry because they drink so much, especially lately. But what really bothers me is how they let me do almost anything I want to do. They never tell me when to come in, and I can go anywhere. You might think how lucky I am. But I tell you that is not how I feel about it. What bothers me is I wonder if I am all that ready to decide everything by myself."

This girl is screaming for guidelines. Yes, it is essential to respect the personhood of our children, to give them room to grow and make decisions, but they can only accomplish this if we lovingly point the way.

There's another kind of privacy that needs to be looked at in family relationships—especially

between parent and child. Too many parents
have a CIA mentality. We are snoops, eaves-
droppers, letter-readers. This can be devastating
to a person of any age. I don't want people
checking out my every activity. Nor do our
children! They want parents who are willing to
be available, yet who aren't snoopers . . . parents
who respect them as human beings and, conse-
quently, do not provoke them to wrath.

*Do I love my child enough to provide firm dis-
cipline?*

Recently at the First Presbyterian Church of
Pittsburgh, we set aside two full Sunday evenings to wrestle with problems in family living.
Blank sheets of paper were given to everyone
in the service. They were invited to write down
any question about family living. Then a panel
of men and women from our staff discussed the
questions. More people raised questions con-
cerning discipline than any other topic.

One prominent writer about family living
warns that a parent should never spank a child.
He speaks strongly against physical punishment. And this becomes understandable when
you know that as a child he was tied to a tree
and whipped by his father. But there is a wide

difference of opinion about discipline and what type of punishment is appropriate. Is it right to apply strong correction to a child? Is spanking permissible?

Proverbs 13:24 reads, "He who spares the rod hates his son, but he who loves him is diligent to discipline him." And the writer of Proverbs goes on to make this tongue-in-cheek statement, "Do not withhold discipline from a child; if you beat him with a rod, he will not die. If you beat him with the rod you will save his life from Sheol" (Prov. 23:13–14).

I personally believe the Bible teaches that we should apply firm discipline to our children. However, James Dobson in his book *Dare to Discipline* warns against going to extremes. On the one hand, some of us are too harsh, totally dominating our children and leaving them in a constant state of fear. On the other hand, some of us are too permissive. Dr. Dobson notes that firm discipline develops respect for a parent, and this is important because it determines all the future relationships of that child's life. He urges that spankings be reserved for a direct expression of self-will when the child says "I will not" in rebellion against the parent's authority. Firm, loving punishment, instead of closing channels of communication, actually opens freedom of expression. Immediately following firm discipline, the average child is most open to expressions of love, understanding, and the warm embrace of the parent.

I can't speak for everyone, but I can for myself. I got plenty of spankings when I was a kid. I didn't like them. I screamed and howled. But they were good for me. They had a way of making me bendable. Dad usually gave the spankings. He'd take us to a little hallway in the center of the house. Five doors entered that hall —causing my bellowing to be insulated from the outside world by the kitchen, bathroom, parents' bedroom, living room, and basement stairway. Dad would always get down on one knee, take off his belt, and say, "Son, you'll never believe me but this spanking is going to hurt me more than you." He was correct. I never believed him. That is until I had to start spanking my own children. It's no fun. Strangely enough though, looking back I wouldn't trade one of those spankings for anything in the world. Perhaps instead there should have been a few more.

One important memory. Dad never spanked me in anger. That's what made the difference. He was in control of himself doing what was his God-given responsibility, applying it as he would say, "to that one part of the human anatomy expressly made for that purpose." Once in anger he slapped my sister across the face. I choke now in emotion as I remember the tears streaming down his face as he asked both Miriam and God to forgive him.

The other evening Anne and I were having dinner with a wonderful Christian couple. Their little five-year-old boy was running wild around the house. They tried to calm him down. He wouldn't. They begged. They threatened. They bribed. Nothing worked. They were scared to give a spanking. As he stuck out his tongue and sassed every adult in the room, his parents were helpless to discipline. It was as if they thought it wasn't Christian to spank. That little fellow was boss around his home. He was literally raising his parents. Perhaps there is a better way to discipline. If you've got one, let me know. I think I've heard them all. Maybe not. At least that little fellow could have used a good hard, loving spanking. It would have worked wonders. A by-product of quick, firm, loving discipline is that you and your children will enjoy each other more. Ultimately, you save on shouting. Your home becomes a more emotionally healthy place.

There are times I am sure when we are afraid that discipline will turn our children against us, but the opposite is true. Failure to discipline is the clear sign that we don't care enough to become vulnerable for their best.

God cares for each of us, and sometimes he disciplines us. Often there is pain in his reproof. In the process, though, he bends us from our way to his way, alerting us to our need of his love, his grace, his authority. God cares that much for us and sets the supreme example of our care for the children entrusted to us.

6
How to Handle Hassles
with Your Parents

Everyone has hassles with his parents. You are not at all different if you've experienced problems. One index to the fact that many people have problems in the child-parent relationship is the number of books recently published on this topic: *Shut Your Generation Gap; Help! I'm a Parent; Do Your Parents Bug You?; Parents on Trial; Living with Parents;* and *How to Raise Your Parents.*

These hassles are not limited to teen-agers;

they go on through adult years. Recently I received a phone call from a young woman in her thirties who was troubled by a problem with her parents. That same day a businessman in his fifties told me about a problem he was having with his father, who had done so much for him but was making demands on his family life. There are all kinds of different problems in the child-parent relationship, and difficulties will always be present.

As a starting point, I urge you to accept a basic Christian truth: As long as you are a human being—subject to sin, living in a world of sinners, relating to parents who also are sinners—there will be problems. However, as Christians, we have the potential to move beyond the bondage of sin to more creative possibilities.

Recently a fourteen-year-old hit me point blank with the comment, "My parents bug me! What can I do about them? They're impossible!" Although I couldn't tell her this, inwardly I had to agree with her. I knew her parents, and they *were* impossible. Her complaint was legitimate; they were bugging her. Her perceptions were reliable. What should I say? Agree with her and leave it at that? No! My young friend had missed the fact that she was part of this problem. Not only were her parents giving her difficulty, she was making life impossible for them. There were some important things that she had not learned about her mother and dad, and only when she learned these, was she set free to experience a much more exciting life-style.

One fact she needed to know was that God created her parents for her benefit. This is a highly significant truth. *Your father and mother, as tough as they are to understand at times, are God's gift to you.* They are part of a chain of command which helps you be the person God intends. In this world there is authority, and this authority is ordered by God. Bill Gothard, in his Institute in Basic Youth Conflicts, refers to this as God's chain of command. The Ten Commandments state, "Honor your father and mother." The Apostle Paul in the New Testament is led by the Holy Spirit to write, "Children, obey your parents in the Lord, for this is right. 'Honor your father and mother' (this is the first commandment with a promise), 'that it may be well with you and that you may live long on the earth'" (Eph. 6:1–3).

Do you catch the positive element of that command? We are to obey, and in the process, we will have a full, positive life. Paul notes that this is the first commandment which gives a promise. The promise is that if we obey, re-

specting the authority of our parents, our life-
style will be blessed of God. Whether this is
simply a psychological fact of life, or whether
God himself goes out of his way to reward you,
is not clearly specified. But I'm inclined to believe it is both, for the Bible is God's clear expression of how to live the life he intended for
us.

On the other hand, the author of the Book of
Proverbs warns of what will happen if we don't
take our parents seriously: "The eye that mocks
a father and scorns to obey a mother will be
picked out by the ravens of the valley and eaten
by the vultures" (Prov. 30:17). In other words,
a person's life is destroyed by failure to obey
God's chain of command.

Now, what is this chain of command? The
Bible teaches that God is able to accomplish his
purpose in our lives through those he places in
authority over us. In the family relationship the
order of authority is God, the human father, the
human mother, and the child. This is not to imply that God intended for the child to be at the
low end of the pecking order and to remain
there. In God's eyes every child is a diamond in
the rough. The father and mother serve as a
hammer and chisel, working to bring out the
finest qualities of the many-faceted potentials

of the young person's personality. Remember, the father and mother work together. The mother is not positioned between father and child in the chain of command. In fact, the father is just as responsible as the mother for the children. And a wise child is willing to be shaped by his parents. If he or she refuses to submit to the sometimes painful experience of being shaped by the authority of God and parents, the young person can end up on the scrap heap, realizing very little of his or her potential.

Another fact my young friend needed to learn is that *God instructs us to obey parents, not to spoil our fun, but because it's smart.* God knows how we function best. He made us, and through his Word he alerts us to a plan for living. He knows that parents have insights which can be of enormous help. How much better it is for the young person to feel open and free enough to take advantage of his parents' experience and judgment. Of course, this is only likely to happen if mother and dad have learned to treat their children as human beings and have established a give-and-take climate in the home.

I'm sure the vast majority of today's teenagers find it virtually impossible to picture their parents as having once been young and facing

similar problems to theirs. It is easy for them
to lose sight of the fact that their parents en-
dured the same feelings of insecurity, frustra-
tions, and problems. Actually this understanding
and communication impasse robs both parent
and child of the benefits of their experience and
opinions. Each can learn from the other if there
is freedom in the relationship.

At this point I feel quite sure that a great
many young people think they already get too
much advice and help from their parents. It's
true—at times we go overboard in our efforts.
One of the best examples of this came through
one night when I was watching the "Odd Couple" on television. Felix Unger is divorced from
his wife, and his daughter was spending the
weekend with him. Felix—a perfectionist, a
pedantic individual—really wanted to be *with*
her, but he turned her off completely by his
phony efforts to identify with her. Instead she
preferred the company of sloppy old Oscar,
Felix's roommate. Why? Simply because he
knew how to identify with her. She wasn't the
least bit interested in ballet, photography, and
music—the things her father enjoyed. So she
went to the ball game with Oscar. While watching the game she developed a crush on one of the
players and decided right then and there she

wanted to be an umpire. So, what did Felix do when he heard about it? He rushed right out and bought her a fancy uniform. This was his desperate way of trying to identify. But he turned her off until she realized that his compulsive and frantic efforts were really based on love.

On the other hand I've talked with young people who have said, "I can't get my dad's time long enough to have a good talk. He's so busy in his work. Mother's so busy with her clubs, her tennis, even her Christian work." In a situation like that Harold Mallet suggests that a young person write a note to his parents and suggests wording it something like this:

Dear folks:

Do you mind if I make a suggestion? We don't talk enough. I realize how much "Go" and "Do" there is in your lives, and I know it's important. But frankly, I need some of your time. It's not that I'm in a jam, or intend to be, but somehow it seems that we belong to different denominations! I go my way and you go yours. We get along fairly well, but I'm like a roomer.

I'd like to discuss dating with you, and some problems that come up about school, parties, drinking, and such. I really need to know what you would say and do.

Could we agree on a time, soon, to fix other times

109

when we can "get with it" more? Yours for the talking!

But in spite of communication and understanding gaps the smart young person in today's complex world will be sensitive to the insights and feelings of his parents. Even the most mixed-up parents have a God-given instinct as to what is best for their children. A few years ago a prostitute came to me for counseling. She had a little five-year-old boy named Mike who had never known his father. The girl was so mixed up; yet she was determined that Michael would not make the same mistakes she had during her teen-age years.

In God's plan, parents are to be obeyed during the growing-up years and respected throughout all of life. You will be a lot happier this way.

But, I've had young people ask, "Is there anything in which God allows me to disobey my parents?"

Yes, I believe there are two contingencies which free a young person from parental authority.

First, *obedience to parents is not valid if their wishes and instructions are in direct opposition to the Word of God—the Bible.* Jesus said, "He who loves father or mother more than me is not worthy of me . . ." (Matt. 10:37). And in another place he said, "Truly, I say to you, there is no man who has left house or wife or brothers or parents or children, for the sake of the kingdom of God, who will not receive manifold more in this time, and in the age to come eternal life" (Luke 18:29–30).

This takes us back to the chain of command idea. God is the ultimate authority over all of life; Jesus Christ should be first. I believe a young person is free to disobey his parents when and if they insist he do something which goes against the Lord. For example, there are some fathers and mothers whose lives are so perverted by sin that they enlist their children's aid in illegal activities. I know parents who have urged their children to steal or lie. And a former associate of mine told me of several young people he knew about whose parents were using them sexually. In such cases, however, it is important for young people to know their Bibles and to seek the counsel of mature Christians.

Second, *you don't have to obey your parents forever*. No, the day comes when you leave father and mother. Maturity means that you have developed in your relationship to God and your fellowman so that you are able to live as an adult. You'll have a new authority relationship—God and his Word. If you are a wife, you will be responsible to your husband as he provides leadership in your home. And the husband is subject to the Lord, finding God's guidance as to the leadership your home needs.

Wise parents guide their children toward independence and then encourage them to move out into responsible living completely free of any thought of obedience to their wishes. I'm sure it's difficult not to meddle. We tend so often to influence or coerce our adult children in one way or another, but this can only produce strain and promote alienation.

One of the most frequent complaints I hear comes from people who say, "I'm an adult, but I still have problems with my parents." Yes, this happens. As long as our parents are alive, they are a part of our lives. They provide enormous joy, but at the same time, there is hurt.

As I see it, two main problems can occur. The first is best expressed in this comment: "My parents are so possessive. They try to dictate my life." I've heard this complaint from people in their twenties, thirties, and forties. One friend of mine went through thirty years of professional life hounded by his father in a business relationship. I know another man in his forties, with a lively brood of teen-age children,

112

who is taking direct instructions from his parents and resenting it all the time. His mother has gone so far as to dictate where he lives and who his friends should be. In the process, he is being torn apart inside.

Frankly, this happens because the child doesn't have the sense really to leave home when he becomes an adult. He may get married. He may live thousands of miles away from father and mother. At the same time, he has left a link of vital connection which keeps him in bondage. Frequently, that link is money. If I, as an adult, am dependent upon my father for my home, for my job, and for an inheritance which someday may come, there is just no way I can avoid a sort of love-hate relationship. I will love him because he's my father, but I'll hate him because of my dependent relationship with him. In a sense I am still a teen-ager dependent upon him, instead of an adult who is self-sufficient, self-governing. Nothing is more pathetic than an adult who is dependent upon his parents for financial and emotional support. If you are caught up in that situation, get out of it. When you leave home, leave home! Love your parents; take them seriously. But don't stay locked into their authority. You have new commitments if you are married, and they demand priority.

The second problem involves in-laws. One psychologist states that 40 percent of the problems during early years of marriage are related to in-law difficulties. He says there are two major causes of this: (1) Parents do not emotionally release their child. (2) The child does not emotionally break away from the parent.

This particular child-parent problem becomes extremely complicated because it involves someone else's parents. There is a strange phenomenon which I have detected in counseling. It's easy for your wife to criticize her own parents and catalog their weaknesses, but if you do it, you're in trouble! Why? Because in reality you have criticized *her* when you thought you were criticizing her parents. She is the product of the people you are criticizing. She expresses her independence when she analyzes them, but she is depersonalized when you analyze them.

The smart in-law is one who gives complete freedom to his son or daughter and family to establish their own lives. This means no financial support, and it means avoiding a bargaining relationship which says, "I'll give you this if you, in turn, do this for me."

On the other hand, the smart young couple realizes that no set of in-laws is perfect. His parents are people; her parents are people. Naturally, they love their son or their daughter. But I believe you can best accept that life if you are free to let it be known that the two of you are primarily committed to each other. You've left your parents to make the husband-wife commitment. In turn, you are going to be loving to the parents of both, yet independent of them. And this independence may require material sacrifices on your part in order to achieve complete emotional freedom.

A child-parent relationship is fraught with potential problems and hassles, but the loving and creative working out of those hassles leads to fulfilling relationships with those who brought us into the world and nurtured us through childhood. The day will come when they are no longer with us. Frank found this out. During his twenties, thirties, and forties he turned on his mother in revenge for her domination during his adolescence. He belittled her, and he ridiculed her life-style. He talked about her behind her back. Then she died. Frank couldn't accept her death. Burdened with guilt he went into severe depression. The mere mention of her name brought tears to his eyes. He had abused a special trust relationship. It was only when he accepted God's forgiveness in Christ that he was set free from his bondage.

Still, he longs to have her back again to express his love and appreciation. He'll never do it in this life. He let his hassles with his mother get the better of him.

7

Facts You Should Know
about Your Partner

Are you puzzled by marriage difficulties? Do you get confused by husband-wife tensions? If so, let's examine some facts which may help you to better understand your partner.

Fact One: *Remember, there is a real difference between a man and a woman.* That may seem like the most insipid statement you've ever read. But while we're very much aware of the physiological differences, I wonder how sensitive we are to the major emotional differences between male and female.

Genesis 1:27 reads, "So God created man in his own image, in the image of God he created him; male and female he created them." Here is a plain and simple statement that both male and female are created in the image of God. And in the second chapter of Genesis, the creation process is given in its sequence. Adam was created first. Then God, seeing Adam's need for a partner, created Eve.

The Scriptures are always clear in pointing toward the distinctiveness of male and female. Both are human beings; yet each has been created different from the other; they are complementary. Genesis 2:24 reads, "Therefore a man leaves his father and his mother and cleaves to his wife, and they become one flesh." The two become one; yet, at the same time, the two are unique, different. There is no way that male and female should be identical, for they maintain a oneness only as they come together.

These days we hear a lot of talk about unisex. This goes against the grain of biblical teaching. While the Bible doesn't say how long a man's hair should be, it does insist that he look like a man. It also says that a woman should look like a woman. A man should cultivate his masculinity, and a woman should assert her femininity. Any effort to blend the sexes into one is wrong, for it destroys what God has created.

Since these differences are so present in us and in every family situation, they require our thoughtful attention. There is every indication today that many of the most critical problems which arise within the husband-wife relationship stem from a lack of understanding of the inherent differences between male and female reactions. What are some of these differences?

First, the male tends to operate on a more logical level, but I add quickly that this is not to imply the female is illogical. It simply means that the male tends to approach living in a more factual fashion while the female tends to respond more emotionally. Of course, it would be wrong to assume that these characteristics can always be defined with black and white clarity. It is wrong to think that every female is all emotion and every male is logical. We all know some women who are much more logical than men. But generally speaking, these characteristics hold true.

Briefly, let's look at some of the other differences. As a rule, the male tends to be more aggressive and open to change. Males are more nomadic. It's easier for a man to uproot himself and relocate in today's mobile society, while a woman is more comfortable with roots firmly fixed in home, friends, and personal relationships.

In many ways I think women are more competitive than men. At least it seems to me the competitive urge is more persistent and deeply felt. This shows up in many ways, but none more vivid than the obvious sizing-up exercise that goes on in a roomful of women—dresses are carefully analyzed as to cost and style. In all fairness, though, I'm inclined to feel that with the advent of more colorful and flamboyant styles in men's clothing, some of this may well be rubbing off on them.

Women tend to be more religious. Possibly this is because of their deeper intuitive strength. Women seem to concentrate on being, while men are more preoccupied with doing. Again, I believe a woman more naturally accepts the supernatural elements which are so much a part of religious faith.

While we've just touched briefly on a few of the differences, these are the stuff out of which marriages are made or broken. I've even simplified to make my point that the two of you are not the same. Even if your emotional fine tuning defies some of these observations, you are still different from your partner. And to illuminate further our ability to understand and handle this important truth, I want to quote Cecil Osborne's rather lighthearted but deeply perceptive comments. He writes that many a woman ". . . desires a father, lover, handyman, and playmate—a kind of composite of John the Beloved, a movie star lover, a businessman with a brief case in one hand and a box of tools in the other, and an all-wise father. This paragon of male virtue must share his life with her, but without boring her with too many details or personal worries which would create insecurity in her. He should be able to meet these needs without neglecting his work."

At the same time, many a husband wants in his partner ". . . an all-forgiving, ever-loving, understanding, wife-mother-mistress; a combination of a mother giving unconditional love, a movie star who is a good housekeeper, a sounding board, an ego builder, an obedient, adoring daughter who thinks his utterances are either profound or quite witty." This quotation is from *The Art of Understanding Your Mate* (Zondervan), a book I recommend highly for every married couple.

Fact Two: *Remember that your marriage will*

have trouble if you allow the distinctly separate husband-wife roles to become blurred. Not only are there emotional and physical differences between male and female, there are also separate functions given to each by God.

The husband is to be the leader in the home. The fifth chapter of Ephesians spells out in detail the kind of relationship the husband and wife are to have, building on the statement "For the husband is the head of the wife as Christ is the head of the church . . ." (Eph. 5:23).

The husband is instructed to love his wife as Christ loves the church. Paul goes on to say, "Even so husbands should love their wives as their own bodies" (Eph. 5:28). He notes that no man hates his own body. That's pretty healthy wisdom. If you can't believe it, go to a men's athletic club. Virile, masculine men pamper themselves with the most delicate attention they can afford. In this Ephesians reference Paul writes that the Christian is to show this same attention and concern for his wife.

The husband is given the primary responsibility to provide for his family's material needs. He must carry the heavy burden of work and the support of the family. This isn't an easy task; the Bible never implies that it is. Quite the opposite, for it teaches that as a result of

124

Adam's sin, man's work will forever be a struggle.

It is also the husband's role to provide for the spiritual welfare of our homes and society. Too often men have abdicated spiritual responsibility in favor of their wives. Nothing is more tragic than a home in which the husband is the spiritual follower. We need men of God, humble in an awareness of sin and need of his forgiveness while at the same time assuming spiritual responsibility for the well-being of their families.

It is equally sad to see a church that is run entirely by women. It is relatively easy for women, with their spiritual sensitivity, to be given the leadership roles in the church. But when this happens, the men either disappear or become passive observers. Women have great abilities, a spiritual sensitivity to be realized in both the home and the church. However, men should never abdicate their leadership role if both the home and the church are to realize their fullest potential.

A further biblical reminder to men is given by Paul as he writes about the importance of husbands always being tender and loving, "Husbands, love your wives, and do not be harsh with them" (Col. 3:19). This is as significant a statement today as when it was first uttered. Masculine brusqueness and even toughness at times can easily result in harshness and insensitivity. Again and again the Bible calls husbands to the high standard of tenderness exemplified in the life and ministry of Jesus Christ.

On the other hand, wives have a different role from that of husbands. The Christian wife is to be adaptable to her husband's leadership. The Scriptures clearly say, "Wives, be subject to your husbands, as to the Lord" (Eph. 5:22).

Submission, however, is more than an outer form. Rather, it is an inner attitude. While some wives outwardly rebel at the idea of submission to their husbands, others seem to go along with it. Many a husband-wife problem emerges because the wife only pretends to be adaptable to the leadership of her husband and inwardly feels resentment and a resistance which comes from denying her own self-will. It does very little good to be outwardly adaptable when you are seething within. One must confront realistically the instinctive resentment toward external authority, whether it be God, parents, employer, civic leader, or husband. We are all subject to authority of one kind or another.

Submission covers us men, also. The same Ephesians 5 that instructs wives to be subject to their husbands also says: "Be subject to one another out of reverence for Christ" (Eph. 5:21). God, in his creation plan, has entrusted us with mutual care, taking responsibilities for each other. I sometimes become most defensive, but ultimately liberated, when Anne confronts me with the shallowness of my logic, the wrongness of my action, or the insensitivity of my dealings with others. Although I am to be the leader in my home, I am also responsible to subject myself to my brothers and sisters in Christ. Anne is one of these sisters, as well as being my wife. This is one place where the chain of command concept breaks down. While my Christian wife is to adapt herself, I must at the same time submit myself to her and the authority of my fellow believers. There is no place for a male autonomy which claims a direct pipeline to God, using this leverage to bend wives and children to a breaking point. In fact, we even have a responsibility to learn from our children. They can be God's vehicle of instruction.

The wife is entrusted with responsibilities for the home. Proverbs 31 illustrates in an agrarian setting the qualities and functions of the Christian woman. She ministers to the needs of her husband and her children. She refuses to let the husband-wife roles become confused, causing her husband to become an "assistant mother." Dr. Bruno Bettelheim, a noted psychologist, warns against the husband being the child-caring agent in the family. He must be a father, not a substitute mother. When these roles are blurred, real problems emerge.

William Westley and Nathan Epstein have done extensive research into discovering the relationship between the mental health of university students and the internal organization of their family background. Their study notes the increase of husband-wife equalitarianism in marriage but suggests that this does not eliminate the need for some system of authority. Conflicts must be resolved, decisions made, and discipline maintained. They note in their book, *The Silent Majority:* "We have found that modern urban families seem to be most successful when they adopt a system of authority that allows for considerable discussion, but in cases of deadlock, allocates the final decision to someone."

Westley and Epstein studied the "power-system" of their test families by evaluating discipline, conflict-resolution, decision-making, and members' impression of which parent dominated. They identified four types of families: father-dominant, father-led, equalitarian, mother-dominant. Equalitarian families are completely democratic, all decisions shared. The husband and wife are equal in authority. Father-led families are also basically democratic. Decisions are arrived at through discussion and usually by consensus. The husband, though, is considered the leader, and he makes the final decision when there is a deadlocked situation.

This empirical study favors a father-led family if the mental health of the children is a premium value. In fact, it has a positive correlation with the mental health of all family members. They conclude: "The father-led type had the largest proportion of emotionally-healthy children, followed by the father-dominant, the equalitarian, and the mother-dominant, in that order. In agreement with most other studies, we found that the mother-dominant form was extremely destructive of family authority and that almost none of the children in these families was emotionally healthy. As far as we could see, these were families with extremely unhappy mothers and cold, impersonal family relationships." *

This kind of research convinces me of the

---

* Westley, William and Epstein, Nathan, *The Silent Majority* (San Francisco: Jossey-Bass, Inc., 1969).

biblical concept of roles. A loving, open, communicative leader-husband-father along with an adaptable, willing-to-be-led wife-mother produces a positive emotional climate. Whereas a leaderless family or a mother-dominant atmosphere not only defies Scripture but tends to produce emotional cripples.

Today we hear a lot about "women's lib." Unfortunately, the Christian church has often been labeled as anti-women's rights. This is far from the truth. The Bible does teach that female dominance in the home or church is wrong and that man is given primary responsibility for leadership. However, the New Testament is a revolutionary document when it comes to the rights of women. Dr. Timothy Smith, professor of history at Johns Hopkins University, has mentioned that probably no historic character has been more falsely interpreted than the Apostle Paul. Paul outlined the responsibility of a woman to be adaptable to her husband, but, inspired by God's Holy Spirit, he also wrote that there is in God's eyes "no male or female." It is helpful to remember that Paul wrote in the context of Hebrew, Greek, and Roman society. With notable exceptions, those societies viewed women as less than human. Few rights were given to them. Both Paul and Christ exploded the concept of women being chattel slaves. Marriage is not two people fighting for their rights, but it is two people understanding that they are only complete together. Theirs is equality in personhood and diversity in roles. While the husband assumes leadership, he is instructed to love his wife as Christ loves the church. This is the epitome of tenderness, sensitivity, graciousness.

It boils down to the practical matter that living in harmony with God's Word is simply the smart way to live. A woman who rebels against her husband's God-given authority is a miserable person. Women are happiest when they are adaptable to the husband's leadership. Wholeness is living the way we were created to live. In part, that's true liberation. I personally believe it is possible to be in bondage to your so-called freedom.

Lest you think I'm a dyed-in-the-wool male chauvinist, let me counter with a few equalizing words for men. We have no right to "lord it over" our wives. They are our crowning glory. We are to display the same sensitivity in our husband-to-wife dealings that Christ shows to us as members of his Church. And we shouldn't be surprised at the outcome. When I'm tender with my wife, it is amazing how graciously she responds to my leadership. When I'm tough and authoritarian, she naturally crawls into her shell, having to fight a legitimate battle with resentment.

God knows what's smart. He's shared it with us. I don't care what books are being written about the "liberated marriage." It's far better to find true freedom in the liberating restraints of God's Word.

My wife, Anne, has urged me to share the way in which her thinking was revolutionized several years ago. She will readily acknowledge that during the first years of our marriage she had a tendency to fight to get her part of the territory. Married to a strong, driving person, she tried to respond in kind, only to find resistance. Then she began to study the Scriptures in preparation to teach a course on the philosophy of Christian womanhood. Here Bible study proved revolutionary. She made radical discoveries about the woman's role, and her whole attitude changed toward me. Instead of fighting for her rights, she began to relax. In the process I relaxed. She had learned something about the male ego, and the complementary relationship in the biblical teaching of roles.

But it is of primary importance for women not to be fearful of their feminine role and by all means men should accept their masculinity.

The Scriptures set out honest and realistic guidelines for both roles.

Fact Three: *Remember, your partner is turned on by your giving of yourself. Next to God, your partner wants to know that he's the most important person in your world.*

Unfortunately, too many of us enter into marriage with a desire to be fulfilled by our partner. Instead, we should come with a desire to fulfill. How quickly the purpose of marriage gets perverted. If we are constantly looking to our partner somehow to release the best that is in us, and if perchance our partner doesn't do this, we point our finger accusingly and say in effect, "You are not a good partner." That act in itself only diminishes his or her capacity to respond to the best that is in us.

Jesus spoke very pointedly about this: ". . . Give, and it will be given to you; good measure, pressed down, shaken together, running over, will be put into your lap. For the measure you give will be the measure you get back" (Luke 6:38). Frequently this verse is used in the context of stewardship, but it does not refer only to the financial support of the work of Christ. Jesus is saying that if you protectively try to get everything for yourself, you will lose. He

133

who wants to be first shall be last; yet if you give yourself away, you will find yourself. The last shall be first; as you give, you shall receive. Desire to fulfill the best in your partner, instead of trying to get your partner to fulfill the best in you.

This is not a manipulative device or a gimmick. Too often we view our partners as objects, not subjects. They, too, are persons and are not ours to "use." The most obvious and despicable play that can be used by either a husband or wife is to do something merely to manipulate the other into thinking or reacting in a desired fashion. A genuine, thoughtful act, designed without self-gain, is certain to speak deeply to the needs of the other person. It may mean arranging for that second honeymoon away from the kids. Or the husband may take a couple of vacation days to paint that room and make repairs around the house. It may mean being more receptive to your partner's sexual drives. And it could well mean holding off on a daily recital about all that went wrong at home until he's had a chance to unwind from his hard and frustrating day at the office. This is somewhat of an awkward way to phrase it, but it says what I mean: Fulfilling instead of being fulfilled will ultimately fulfill you the most.

Your partner wants to know that next to God he or she is the most important person in the world to you. There's a fascinating phrase in the Bible that I think we've not mastered. It reads, "Therefore a man leaves his father and his mother and cleaves to his wife, and they become one flesh" (Gen. 2:24). A man is literally to leave his father and mother and become *one* with his wife.

But so often after marriage this oneness is diluted because one or both partners begin to give priority to the children which come along. If we're not careful we can, over a period of time, find happening to us what happened to Joan and Bill. They had an exciting marriage until the kids came. Then Joan made the kids the most important part of her life. For twenty-five years she devoted herself entirely to her three children. And when the last one got married, Joan was all alone with Bill. To their amazement they discovered they no longer really knew each other.

Joan had failed to understand that while she was committed to Christ through eternity and she was committed to her partner until "death do us part," her commitment to her children essentially was only for as long as they were at home. Sad is the parent who cannot let the children go—whose security is based on them alone. When children are put first by either parent, the husband-wife relationship suffers immeasurably.

It can also warp the children. I think of Mary, twenty-two years old, who just broke an engagement because she couldn't relate to men. Why? Because her father had carried on a twenty-two year romance with daughter Mary—not with Mary's mother. He had doted on her and had created a compulsive and dependent relationship. As a result she has all kinds of hang-ups.

On the other hand, if Mary's father had channeled those same energies into the husband-wife relationship, he could have loved his daughter and spent time with her without leaving room for her to feel, even unconsciously, that she was in competition with her mother for her father's love.

We are going to lose our children. Thank God we do. We give them away. They are to be whole, healthy people, able to commit themselves to someone else. And when they do, it will be a joyous and fulfilling time because of our total commitment to our partner in marriage who next to God is the most important person in our lives.

8

Problems—
Every Healthy Marriage
Has Them

Does your marriage have problems? I hope so! Actually, there is no such thing as "a perfect marriage." To have a perfect marriage you would have to have two perfect people, and I don't know of anyone who can bear that label. Even the best marriage has its problems simply because people have problems, and marriages are made up of people.

Some couples with whom I talk in premarital counseling sessions probably consider me a "killjoy." We spend considerable time discussing a list of problems, some of which every marriage will have.

The average engaged couple has difficulty taking these sessions seriously. Their eyes are aglow with love, and they're excited about the forthcoming wedding. Often I hear them say, "Isn't it amazing how much we have in common? . . . how we enjoy the same things? . . . how much we think alike?" Little do they realize that a few short weeks after the marriage—if they would honestly admit their feelings—they might instead say something like this, "Isn't it amazing how different we are? . . . how unalike we think? . . . how dissimilar our responses to life?" One minister friend of mine has completely stopped premarital counseling. Instead, he requires that each couple he plans to marry agree prior to their wedding to *post*marital counseling. He has discovered they are much more receptive to objective discussions after a few weeks of marriage than they were before the wedding.

Let's take a closer look at just a few of the potential problems which every marriage faces.

One is *differences in family background*. No two people come from an identical home environment. Adjustments in this area might be minimal—if the couple grew up in the same town, went to the same school, attended the same church, joined the same clubs, and had fathers engaged in similar employment. This is seldom the case in our increasingly mobile world. Art meets Karen in college. She's from the Northeast; he's from the Midwest. She's an Episcopalian; he's a Methodist. Her father is vice-president of a bank; his is a foreman in a factory. Art and Karen grow to love each other very much. In the neutral setting at the university they seem alike. They dress similarly, enjoy the same type of entertainment, and are majoring in similar subjects. The university serves as a melting pot, bringing them together in a oneness. She meets his parents; he meets hers. They become engaged and get married.

Then come the problems. Karen was raised with unlimited credit cards at her disposal; Art doesn't believe in credit cards. His family had to pay cash on the line to make sure they had enough money to make ends meet. Karen loves the liturgy of her Episcopal church; Art prefers the more simple worship of the Methodist church. Karen's mother wants her to become a member of the Junior League; Art's family has never even heard of the organization. Karen prefers gourmet cooking while Art likes Southern fried chicken with mashed potatoes and

141

gravy. Art and Karen love each other very much, but they're very different and these differences can cause trouble.

Closely allied with differences in family background are problems with *in-laws*. Among the major crises in a newlywed's life is deciding at which parents' home they will spend their first Christmas. Little did they anticipate that this could be a problem. Both families are sentimental about holidays and have their timeworn customs. Both naturally envision the couple opening their gifts with them around their Christmas tree. Art and Karen now live in Chicago. Do they go to her parents in Boston, breaking their backs financially, or do they go to his parents in Peoria? Do they accept the two plane tickets from her parents in Boston, or do they limp down to his parents' place in their beat-up old VW? Seems like a small thing? Of course! But when it comes to in-laws, small problems like this become gigantic.

Then there's the problem of *money*. Every couple has either too little or too much. It may seem a bit difficult to imagine any couple having too much. Come to think of it, I don't think I've ever talked with a couple who thought they had too much. Anyway, the important thing is how you handle what you have. What gets the priorities—a new car or a bedroom suite? Who handles the checkbook? Do you have separate checking accounts? If so, do you both keep them straight and always remember to enter the check when you write it? Every person has a money personality. Either you're a spendthrift or a miser. That may seem an exaggeration, but it really isn't because two misers married to each other will not be identical in their miserly ways. One is certain to seem like a spendthrift to the other.

As important and wonderful as it is, nothing can cause more trouble than *religion*. Deciding what church to attend can become a real bone of contention, not only between married couples but between their families. Frequently, even grandparents get into the act and put pressure for their grandchildren to be raised in a Baptist church while grandparents on the other side are laying it on for the Methodist church.

Then there's *temperament*. He enjoys ski trips while she wants to stay home and sew. She likes parties; he prefers a quiet evening in front of the fireplace with a book. She talks a lot and is outgoing; he's introverted and shy.

And then there's the problem of *children*. How many? How do we raise them? One partner insists on being strict while the other wants their child to have the same kind of carefree, happy youth he or she did.

Of course, these are just a few of the many problems that can arise within the marriage relationship. And it may come as a bit of a surprise to some, but every couple has the same problems in one form or another. It's inevitable. The question really is not will we have them, but how do we cope.

The difference between a healthy and unhealthy marriage is that in a healthy marriage the couple acknowledges that they have problems, knowing that with Christ's help nothing is too big to handle. Problems don't have to break up a marriage. In fact, problems can be the stabilizing, cohesive factor which will cement a marriage together with greater firmness.

Jesus said, "In the world you will have trouble." He voiced this sophisticated understanding of the nature of man, both within society at large and within the husband-wife relationship. Jesus warned his followers that this world is not an easy place in which to live. And he was quick to bring into focus a realistic look at human nature, seeing implications for today in the sinful rebellion of Adam and Eve.

It is fascinating to discover that Jesus didn't couple a pessimistic spirit with his realistic understanding of life. Instead he called his followers to hope: "But take courage, I have overcome the world." In this spirit Jesus talked about marriage, pointing out the sanctity of the husband-wife relationship. Quoting from Genesis when questioned about the permissibility of divorce, Jesus said, "Have you not read that he who made them from the beginning made them male and female, and said, 'For this reason a man shall leave his father and mother and be joined to his wife, and the two shall become one'? So they are no longer two but one. What therefore God has joined together, let no man put asunder" (Matt. 19:4–6). Jesus was quick to understand that the sinful nature of all men and women could inevitably corrupt the husband-wife commitment. He acknowledged that this sin could so affect the man-woman relationship that in extreme circumstances the two people would no longer live together. Yet Jesus viewed divorce as an absolute last resort, permissible only in the most extreme cases of infidelity and desertion.

In contemporary words *Jesus was warning against* the use of the term *incompatibility*. This is a deadly word and an incredible cop-out. We've already agreed that every marriage has its problems because no one is perfect. But present marriage statistics indicate that too many couples, when confronted with the normal routine problems of marriage, throw up their hands and say, "Well, I guess we are just incompatible." And they head for the closest divorce court.

Swiss psychiatrist Paul Tournier suggests that we exorcise the word *incompatibility* from our vocabulary. In his book entitled *To Understand Each Other* he says, "So-called emotional incompatibility is a myth invented by jurists short of arguments in order to plead for divorce. It is likewise a common excuse people use in order to hide their own feelings. I simply do not believe it exists. There are no emotional incompatibilities. There are misunderstandings and mistakes, however, which can be corrected where there is the willingness to do so."

Adjustments in marriage are necessary. There must be honest give-and-take from both sides of the relationship. Judson and Mary Landis in their book *Building a Successful Marriage* bring into focus three basic forms of adjustments.

First, there is the adjustment of compromise. Here a husband and wife seek together to find a middle ground of agreement satisfactory to both. This means that neither party is called

146

upon to give too much . . . one person isn't expected to make all the concessions.

The second type of adjustment is required when a couple discovers they have seriously opposing viewpoints or antagonistic characteristics. Instead of fighting each other throughout all of life, they learn to accommodate themselves to their differences. An entirely satisfactory compromise may not always emerge, but an accommodation is achieved because of their deep love for each other. A mutually acceptable balance is found which removes most of the strain.

A third form of adjustment is to settle into a state of hostility. Constant quarreling and bickering go on at the points where the husband and wife differ. Tension is produced by antagonisms that are sometimes expressed in words and often made even clearer by their behavior. Unable to cope with their differences, the couple reach an impasse—a static, inflexible solidifying of the relationship which is marked by hostility.

Even the healthiest marriage has its problems, but two mature and caring people will refuse to let them solidify. Concerted effort is made toward adjustments, with each person bending over backwards to understand the feelings of

147

the other. Love is cultivated and nurtured even when there are seemingly irreconcilable differences of attitude and temperament. This couple realizes that marriage is a relationship between two adults. It's not for teen-agers. What if your fourteen-year-old daughter came to you with stars in her eyes and said, "Mommy, I've found the perfect guy. I want to get married!" What would you do? In one way or another you'd get the fact across that she is still a child. She isn't ready for marriage. Unfortunately, many adults are still teen-agers emotionally. If we're going to have vital marriages, we must approach them as adults, realizing that maturity is the capacity to postpone immediate gratification for the ultimate good. *We can develop a love relationship by looking to the well-being of our partner instead of our own personal happiness.*

The Apostle Paul strips away all of our sentimental phony definitions of love as he writes, "This love of which I speak is slow to lose patience—it looks for a way of being constructive. It is not possessive: it is neither anxious to impress nor does it cherish inflated ideas of its own importance.

"Love has good manners and does not pursue selfish advantage. It is not touchy. It does not keep account of evil or gloat over the wickedness

148

of other people. On the contrary, it is glad with all good men when truth prevails.

"Love knows no limit to its endurance, no end to its trust, no fading of its hope; it can outlast anything. It is, in fact, the one thing that still stands when all else has fallen" (1 Cor. 13:4–8, Phillips).

This penetrating definition of love is an antidote to incompatibility. It helps you adjust yourself to your partner, and it will strip away self-pity, grudge-holding, and the petty criticisms which destroy the husband-wife relationship. It bases itself on the New Testament understanding of love which is so different from the contemporary ideal. This is the love Christ showed for his church and the love a husband and wife are to show to each other. It is unconditional love.

Believe me, a couple willing to love this way is set free from the incompatibilities which can destroy a marriage. It involves being faithful even when your partner fails to live up to his responsibilities. It is important to realize that I don't have to wait for my partner to be perfect. That's not going to happen anyway, but I can act and react properly because I know that is God's will for my life. The attitude which says, "I'll shape up when he does and not one minute sooner" doesn't square with God's pattern. Instead I think he would prefer we say, "I don't fully understand why he acts that way, but with your help, Lord, I'm going to be a faithful, loving, sensitive wife no matter what." Men need to be just as patient: "Lord, keep me steady in my love for her, standing by her no matter what she does. Help me to fulfill my covenant of faithfulness." That attitude certainly pulls the rug out from under the incompatibility idea. In fact, Peter writes to women who have inconsiderate non-Christian husbands saying, "Likewise you wives, be submissive to your husbands, so that some, though they do not obey the word, may be won without a word by the behavior of their wives, when they see your reverent and chaste behavior" (1 Peter 3:1–2). Simply stated, Peter is saying that your willingness to view marriage, not as a fifty-fifty proposition, but as a 100 percent giving on your part will set into action revolutionary spiritual laws, which in many cases can bring to life a dead relationship.

There are four words that I think are important to every marriage. Let's examine them briefly.

Word One: *Triangle*. A healthy marriage is a triangle affair, involving a husband and a wife and a third party—Jesus Christ. As we allow him to be part of our relationship, we are certain to find a healthy oneness with our marriage partner. Our lives must constantly be open to Jesus Christ, admitting our mistakes, and asking his forgiveness. As we spend time alone with him each day, we find release and strength. Then the Bible becomes an open and alive book, and the Holy Spirit will guide us into creative relationships. The Lord wants our marriages to succeed and be happy.

Word Two: *Commitment.* Remember that marriage is meant to be permanent. Remind yourself periodically of those marriage vows which said in effect that no matter what you do to me or no matter what life throws at us, I will be faithful to you until death. That certainly covers all the ups and downs of marital life. It handles the emotional upsets. It is the greatest and most significant of all contracts, and it's worth keeping even when you don't feel like it. And there are times when the best people don't feel like it.

Word Three: *Communication.* Nothing puts a couple more at ease than to know that they are communicating. Even differences of opinion can be joyously expressed when there is an honest, nonhostile grappling with diversity. Some of the greatest times in our marriage are when Anne and I, discovering that we have allowed daily events to push us apart, sit down and talk and listen. We air our differences and ask the Lord to forgive us. In this climate we are able to wrestle creatively with how we can improve our marriage. We plan together, laugh together, cry together. That's communication. It is painful at times because it involves complete honesty, but honesty is basic to communication.

Anne has just read this paragraph. Her response was, "John, is that all you're going to say about communication?"

I was immediately defensive, retorting, "I've tried to weave it all the way through the book."

"Fine, but you haven't shared how really painful and liberating this concentrating on communication has been for us."

I guess I haven't. We've talked about the importance of keeping genuine doors of conversation open with partner, children, and parents. But Anne is correct—real communication is some of the most painful joy possible. Come to think of it, is there anything worthwhile that isn't painful?

Anne and I have had a story-book romance. We met in Formosa while she was on the way to Cambodia to teach for a summer between her junior and senior years at UCLA. I was a middler at Princeton Theological Seminary, working my way through school in the travel business. I fell in love with her at first sight. There was only one problem—she barely saw me because she was in the process of becoming engaged to another fellow. But five months later, she and her fiancé broke up of natural causes. By this time she was back in Los Angeles and I was at Princeton. Two months later we had our first date, and a month after that we were engaged. Five months later we were married. We knew it was the Lord's will, and our parents agreed, even though we had actually been together a total of six weeks.

After a modest five-day honeymoon, we settled into a summer assistant pastorate in Palmdale, California, before the last year of seminary. And then the get-acquainted process began as we started to blend two very different temperaments, from two very different—although both Christian—home backgrounds.

A missionary couple had warned us to "never let the sun go down on your wrath." There were some nights that the sun didn't set until two or three the next morning. All our love and absolute assurance that God had brought us together didn't ease the pain of totally honest communication.

More than a decade later, we are still learning lessons in communication—and are much the richer for it. We don't stay up quite so late any more. I've learned not to be so compulsive and demanding in my communication. We've learned to respect each other's periodic need for silence, and we're beginning to get beyond the exhausting introspective talk which both dominated and frustrated some of those earlier verbal marathons. We're trying to work more at sharing ideas—concentrating on discoveries from our reading and daily experience. But there is still friction now and then and periodic moments of defensiveness as we make ourselves vulnerable to each other. However, we'll both swear by the fact that the pain is worth it, as we share our deepest fears and aspirations—still getting to know each other.

For a moment, let's talk about sex. We've not said too much about this. If you're trying to use sex to get a beautiful marriage—forget it! A beautiful, growing marriage is what produces good sex. Again, it's a matter of communication. When you're communicating, sex is better —not the other way around. I've always counseled courting or engaged couples to hold off on praying too much together when they are alone. Why? Because conversation and sincere prayer

154

mix into the best lubricant for intercourse. What makes holding back so tough before marriage is what can revolutionize your sex life.

It's almost a cliché to say it, but that doesn't make it less true—a happy and fulfilled sex life hinges on attitude. Are you really convinced that anything goes between two married people which is neither physically injurious or personally distasteful to one or both of you? Are you willing to experiment with each other in every area of life, finding that psychic-spiritual "turn-on" that produces good sex? Do you concentrate on bringing joy to your partner, more than joy to yourself?

Don't expect to remain free in a fun sex relationship if you are not having a rewarding friendship together in other areas of your relationship. Anne and I are all for sex above the covers with candles. And she has just urged me to encourage you gals to an open-minded experimentation. Don't hesitate to initiate some sex play. Don't always wait for him. He needs you every bit as much as you need him. But we've both found that all the gimmicks are subject to the law of diminishing returns if we are not really *one*. Not that we've fully arrived—possibly we never will—but we're striving together towards wholeness.

155

Word Four: *Humor*. A sense of humor is absolutely essential to a creative marriage. I'm referring here to the capacity to laugh at yourself, not at your partner. I find this quality indispensable to all of my activities. Like most people I tend to take myself too seriously—just another way of spelling pride. If you can laugh at yourself, you may be able to tolerate a chuckle or two from your partner as together, with the Lord's help, you shape a relationship for the future.

How does one end a book like this? Perhaps it is best to conclude with a prayer. Here is one that means a great deal to me and has helped more than once as I have tried to be the right kind of a husband and father. Will you pray it with me? "Dear God, I love you. I need you. I'm sorry for my sin. I'm sorry for not being all I should be to my family, and I claim your forgiveness. I want to be your person. I place my trust in Jesus Christ who died for my sins and rose from the dead as victor. Empower me now to make the contribution which will get my family off to a fresh start. Help me to do what I can to encourage my family toward greater wholeness. In the name of Jesus Christ my Savior. *Amen*."